It's About Time

Designed to help drummers and other musicians understand, control, and improve their sense of time

by Fred Dinkins

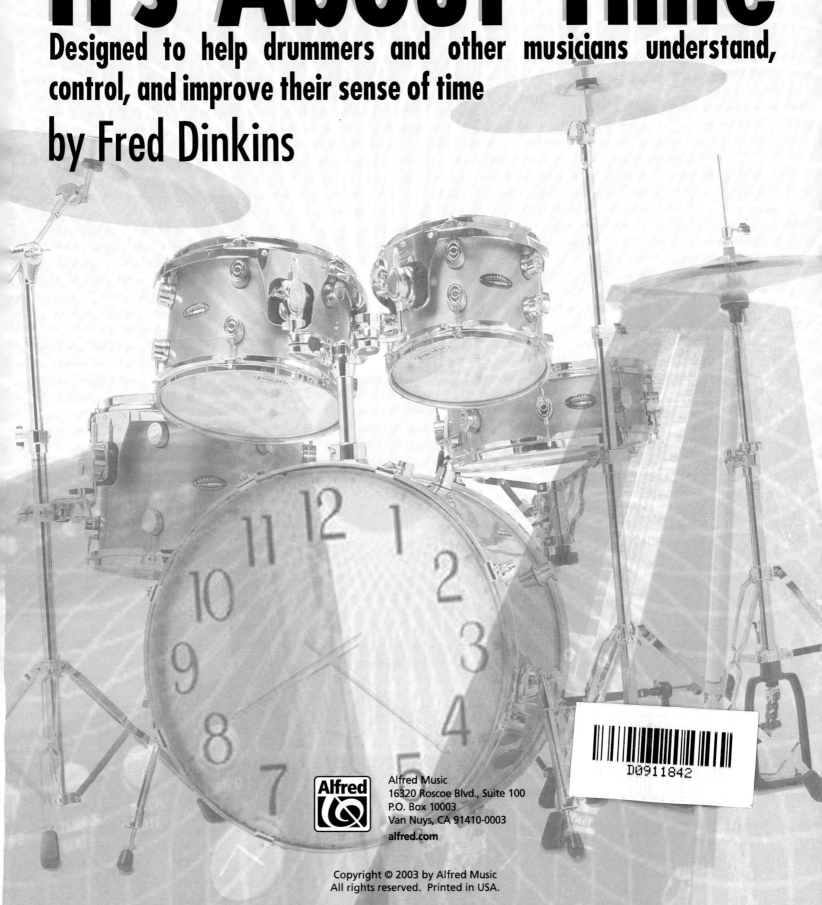

Alfred Music
16320 Roscoe Blvd., Suite 100
P.O. Box 10003
Van Nuys, CA 91410-0003
alfred.com

ISBN-10: 0-7579-1410-1
ISBN-13: 978-0-7579-1410-2

D0911842

It's About Time

Designed to help drummers and other musicians understand, control, and improve their sense of time

by Fred Dinkins

■

Project Manager
Ray Brych

■

Editor
Joe Testa, Ed Uribe

■

Additional Editing
Don Meagher, Ray Brych

■

Technical Editing
Nadine DeMarco

■

Photography
Mildred Dinkins and Gerald Rodriguez

■

Cover Design
Fred Dinkins, Ken Oefelein and Dancing Planet® MediaWorks™

■

Book Design and Layout, Music Typesetting
Dancing Planet® MediaWorks™

■

Audio Recording, Mixing, and Mastering
Fred Dinkins and Leonard Jones

■

Music Composed and Performed by:
Fred Dinkins, John Barnes, Greg Moore, Dwayne "Smitty" Smith, Reggie Hamilton, Nick Smith, Del Atkins, Danny Diaz, David Leach, Richie Garcia

■

Music Pre-production Assistants:
Tony Coleman, Leonard Jones, Todd Shoemaker, Clarence Allen, Orlando Rashid

Table of Contents

Foreword

by Harvey Mason

Fellow Musicians,

The *It's About Time* method is a guaranteed solution to time problems. Many years ago, I experimented with this concept and found it to be a proven method for improvement and confidence. Fred has worked tirelessly to perfect this approach and he has finally produced this book, which I fully endorse. If used consistently, *It's About Time* will cure rushing, dragging, and confidence problems and will provide stability to your musical vocabulary. This method will definitely work!

Fred with Harvey Mason

Fred demonstrating the 2 and 4 pocket during a clinic for Allegro Music in Santa Fe, New Mexico

About the Author

Fred Dinkins was born in St. Louis, Missouri, and at the early age of six began swinging his first pair of sticks. By the age of 13, he began his professional career playing with various gospel acts.

In 1982, he moved to Los Angeles, California, with his family to expand his musical education. Shortly thereafter, Fred became a teacher at the world-famous Musicians Institute, Percussion Institute of Technology (PIT). His unique style of teaching good time-keeping and grooving has earned him recognition as one of PIT's most sought-after teachers and clinicians.

Fred has performed with saxophonist Sam Riney, gospel great Andrae Crouch, the Emotions, Edwin Hawkins, Kurt Whalum, Paul Jackson Jr., Norman Brown, Barbara Morrison, Hugh Masakela, and many others.

Fred's recording credits include Tramaine Hawkins' Grammy-nominated and Dove Award-winner "What Shall I Do" from *The Joy That Flood My Soul* album, the O'Neal Twins' Grammy-nominated *Blessed Boulevard*, and Debbie Allen's Broadway musical ballet soundtrack *Soul Possessed*.

Some of his video and television credits include *Blackstreet, You Are My Joy, The American Dream, Documentary of the Jackson 5*, Jerry Lewis's 1998 *MD Telethon, Good Morning America* with the Emotions, Sinbad's *Funkfest in Aruba* for HBO, Verdine White's *Rhythm of the Earth* bass instructional video, and *Dick Clark's 50th American Bandstand Anniversary* with 2002 Taste of Honey seen on VH1. He was also the drummer and producer of *The Emotions Live*.

Throughout the year, Fred tours with the Emotions as drummer and musical director, Denise Williams, and other artists. When home, he can be found teaching at PIT or in a session at Intersound Production Studios working for producer John Barnes, as well as on numerous other projects.

You can contact Fred via his Web site at: www.freddinkins.com.

Fred with Marvin "Smitty" Smith

Mentors Harvey Mason and Ricky Lawson with Fred

Acknowledgments

I would like to say praise God from whom all blessings flow. Thanks for the gift and talent to play, hear, and perform this gift of music.

This work is dedicated to my beautiful and caring wife Mildred. Thank you for your love and patience with me for 28 years. To my children Fred Antoine and Shaniece Nicole, and my mother Mrs. Willie Mae Dinkins: thank you for all of your support from birth. To my late father Ulysses Dinkins, my sisters, brothers, in-laws, nieces, nephews, the Boyd family, V. Austin, D. & L. Bader, Larry & Donna Seals, Alvin Hayes and family, and Marvin "Smitty" and Kim Smith.

Spiritual Leader
My Pastor Bishop Kenneth C. Ulmer: thank you for the Word; thank you for helping me to keep the faith and to never give up.

Music Educators
Efrain Toro, Maria Martinez, Chuck Flores, Chuck Silverman, Steve Houghton, Gary Hess, Ralph Humphrey, Ralph Razze, bassist George Lopez, Richard Wilson, and Joe Porcaro, Laval Belle

Music Mentors
Mr. Harvey Mason, Ricky Lawson, Ndugu Chancler, Dennis Chambers, Mike Clark, Gerry Brown, and Joe Porcaro, Marvin "Smitty" Smith.

Personal Industry Friends
Richie Garcia, Curt Bisquera, Clayton Cameron, Michael White, Michael Baker, Freddie White, Rayford Griffin, Ralph Johnson, Eddie Roscetti, Sonny Emory, Will Kennedy, Daryl Woolfolk, Kazuhiro, Gail Johnson, Paul Richardson, and Casey Scheurrell.

Personal Mentoring
Thanks to the following: Papa Joe Porcaro for taking me under your wing, for I would not have made it this far without both you and your wife; William "Bubba" Bryant for the push; Land Richards, for always encouraging me; John Barnes, for being a great human being; Harvey Mason, for all the great music and lessons on drumming and life; Wanda Vaughn and the Emotions band members; Marvin "Smitty" Smith, for the lessons and constant friendship; Dennis Chambers, for the music and constant encouragement; and Ricky Lawson, for just being Ricky; you're the best.

Project Contributors
A very special thanks to Harvey Mason, Dennis Chambers, Ricky Lawson, Marvin "Smitty" Smith, Land Richards, Doane Perry, Gerry Brown, and John Barnes. My deepest thanks to my daughter (my princess) for all of her help.

Performances
Tony Coleman, Nick Smith, John Barnes, Sole Brewer, Reggie Hamilton, Greg Moore, Dwayne "Smitty" Smith, Paul Jackson, Jr., Del Atkins, Danny Diaz, and David Leach.

Special Tributes
My belated sister and brothers Mrs. Eva Gray, Mr. Curry Mitchell, and Mr. Ernest K. Mitchell; my musical brothers, Jeff Porcaro and Carlos Vega; my belated friends, Rev. J. E. Turner, L. D. Richardson and Neely Dinkins.

Instrument Contributions
Sabian Cymbal Co. (Andy Zildjian, Bobby Boos, Wayne Blanchard, and Dom Famularo), Vater Percussion (Alan Vater, Ron Vater, and John Dawkes), DW Drum Pedals (Scott Donnel), H.Q. Percussion Products (Rob B. Jim), Spaun Snares (Brian and David), Shure Microphones (Jack Kotney and Ryan Smith), Extreme Isolation Headphones (John Gresko), Remo Drums, Heads, and Percussion (Chris Hart, Gavin Carignan, and Matt Connors), Hart Dynamics, Jerry Antonelli at Digidesign, Mark Spivak at West L.A. Music, Mark Tippon at Aphex Systems, Lorey and Eric Pershing of Spectrasonics, Greg Tease at E-Magic, Denise Atkins at Glyph Drives, and John and Helen Ellinger of Mibac Music Software.

Project Overseers
A very special thanks to Michael Finkelstein and David Hakim at Warner Bros. Publications for believing in this project and for giving me the chance; to Ray Brych for all of his help, and to Doane Perry for the introduction to Mr. Fink. Last but not least, Joe Testa and Ed Uribe, for all the wisdom and knowledge that went into this project.

Fred helping a student understand that "It's About Time"

Introduction

Welcome to *It's About Time*. When you play with other musicians, do you ever hear statements such as "don't rush," "don't drag," "play in the pocket," and "watch the time when you play your fills"? If you're like most drummers, the answer is "YES." It was my desire to hear FEWER of these kinds of statements that motivated me to develop many of the exercises in this book. These exercises are specifically designed to help you improve, control, and better understand your sense of time.

The way we feel time is influenced by the music we practice, play, and listen to. This can be both good and bad, depending on habits we have developed. The exercises in this book will help identify and reverse bad habits so you can begin contributing to the ultimate goal—developing consistent time. Once this is achieved, you can "move" the time appropriately for all the right musical reasons. Knowing when and how to adjust your time intentionally can sometimes be the difference between merely playing notes and actually performing music. When used properly, *It's About Time* will help you control wanted and unwanted movements in your playing.

With such a large amount of material, it may be easy to get diverted from the book's main purpose. Therefore, when first going through the book, try to practice the exercises exactly the way they are laid out. As you dig further into the subject material and become more familiar with each chapter's purpose, you will begin creating your own ideas for practicing. Eventually, you will get to the point where you practice each chapter in conjunction with one another and, thereby, fully maximize the potential of this book.

The CD that accompanies the book has important practice tools to be used with many of the exercises. Due to the limited amount of space, only so many tempos could be utilized on the CD. Individual loops are available for download at www.freddinkins.com. Once you master each of the exercises utilizing the tempos on the CD, then duplicate the concepts at various tempos with help from TNT 2 software. The more tempos at which these exercises are practiced, the better the results you will see in your playing.

Included at the end of the book is a list of Musical Recommendations. These are to help you increase your listening library and reinforce the subject matter outside the practice room. To develop good time, you should not only practice it, but also live it.

As a final note, keep in mind that this book was written with the understanding that the student already has a basic understanding of basic rhythm and note values. Though it is not absolutely necessary, I highly recommend that you have a good teacher to work with as you study the exercises in this book.

It is my hope that you enjoy practicing and working with the exercises in *It's About Time*. Understanding and mastering your time should involve a combination of hard work and fun. Good luck and have fun!

Best wishes,

Fred Dinkins

Notation Key

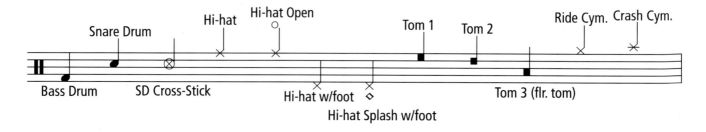

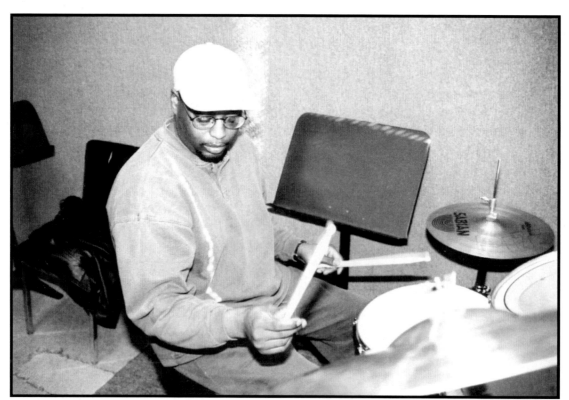

Fred working in his teaching studio

Chapter 1

Grooving With Independence

The most common obstacle in developing good time is the lack of a strong independence vocabulary. It is essential to develop good independence between all four limbs and your voice. The slightest delay or anticipation in any one limb can cause the time of any beat to "stutter" or "hiccup," which will in turn cause a hesitation or disruption in the groove. The best way to avoid these disruptions and develop good independence is to perform as many limb combinations as possible. This takes a good amount of practice but, in time, the communication between the brain and muscles becomes more familiar, and the movement between limbs becomes more natural. This increases your independence vocabulary causing the hesitations and delayed reactions among the limbs to lessen. Developing a good independence vocabulary is the first step towards improving time and groove.

There are many books and videos that focus only on the development of independence. I recommend that you practice with as many of these materials as possible. The more independence mastered by your brain, muscles, and limbs, the better.

The Fifth Limb

The first step to building your independence vocabulary is developing what I like to call the Fifth Limb. In a fun way, your ability to vocalize while playing can be considered an additional "limb" to your hands and feet, simply by counting the subdivisions out loud while you play each exercise. Though this may seem weird to do at first, do not take it lightly. Counting out loud will assist you in developing an internal clock and will help build a foundation for your independence vocabulary.

Choosing what to verbalize depends on the tempo of the groove but, in most cases, the smallest or basic subdivision is the best. For example, if the tempo is very fast, vocalizing all the sixteenth-note subdivisions may not be feasible; however, in a slow tempo, it works perfectly.

The following exercises are to help you strengthen your Fifth Limb. While playing, you have to think of the basic subdivisions of the groove while verbalizing the specific subdivision shown above each exercise. Remember to practice ALWAYS with a click or metronome. On the CD, I perform one example of each subdivision type, so you can get an idea of what it should sound like when you first practice these exercises.

1. Sixteenth-Note Subdivision Grooves

For the following exercises, it is best for you to THINK all the sixteenth-note subdivisions (such as 1-e-&-a 2-e-&-a 3-e-&-a 4-e-&-a) but to VERBALIZE only what is indicated.

a) Quarter-Note Grooves

Sixteenth-Note Subdivision Grooves *(continued)*

As in the previous exercises, it is best for you to THINK all the sixteenth-note subdivisions (such as 1-e-&-a 2-e-&-a 3-e-&-a 4-e-&-a) but to VERBALIZE only what is indicated.

b) Eighth-Note Grooves

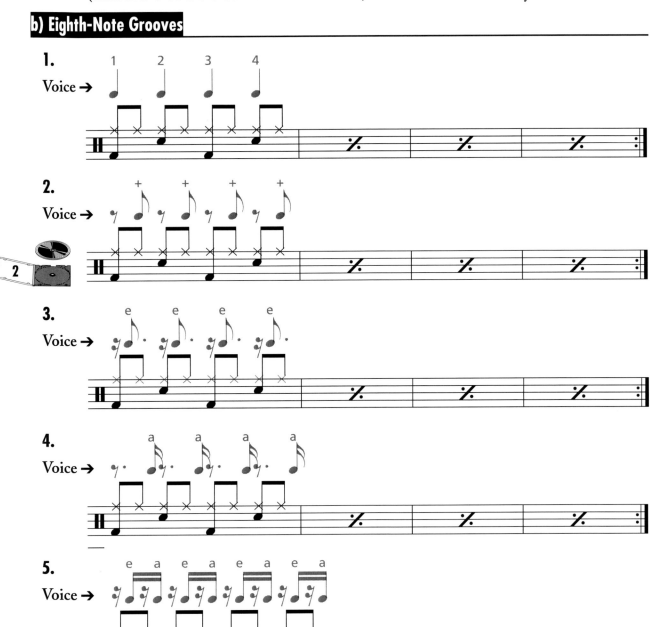

Sixteenth-Note Subdivision Grooves (*continued*)

Again, continue to THINK all the sixteenth-note subdivisions (such as 1-e-&-a 2-e-&-a 3-e-&-a 4-e-&-a) but to VERBALIZE only what is indicated.

2. Eighth-Note Triplet Subdivision Grooves

For the following exercises, it is best for you to THINK all the triplet subdivisions (such as 1-trip-let 2-trip-let 3-trip-let 4-trip-let) but to VERBALIZE only what is indicated.

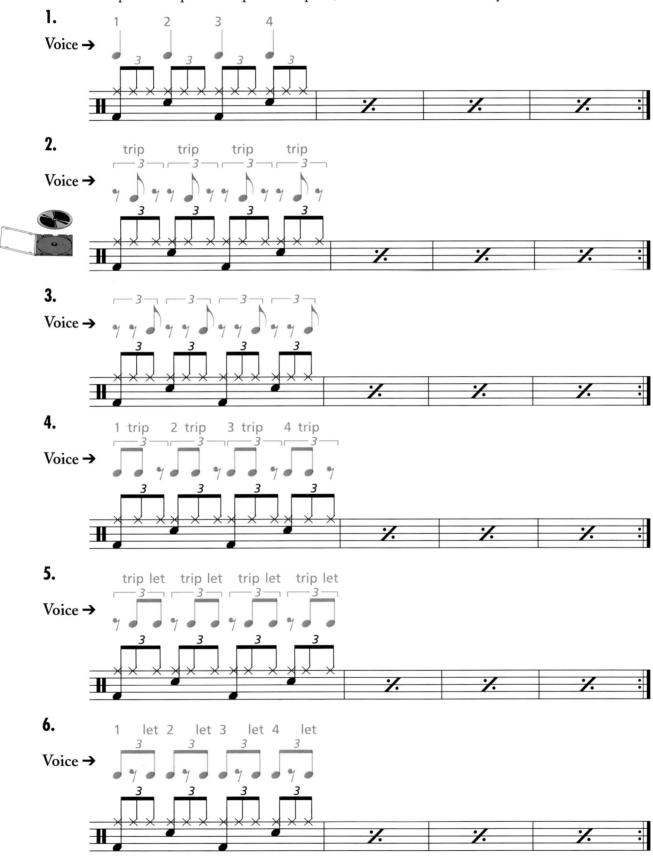

Adding the Fourth Limbs

Now that you have increased your inner clock with your Fifth Limb, it is time to begin working on your other four limbs. Remember, just as you should always use a click when practicing, so should you also always use your Fifth Limb.

Three-Limb Ostinatos (TLO)

There are 30 TLOS that incorporate both hands and the left foot. It is important to be able to play these before adding the fourth limb: the right foot.

The Fourth Limb Patterns (FLP)

Once you have mastered the TLOs by themselves, move on by adding the Fourth Limb. There are 84 FLPs for the right foot (bass drum). Practice each TLO with each FLP until you have practiced every combination. On the CD, you will hear various combinations as examples.

TLO (Three-Limb Ostinatos)

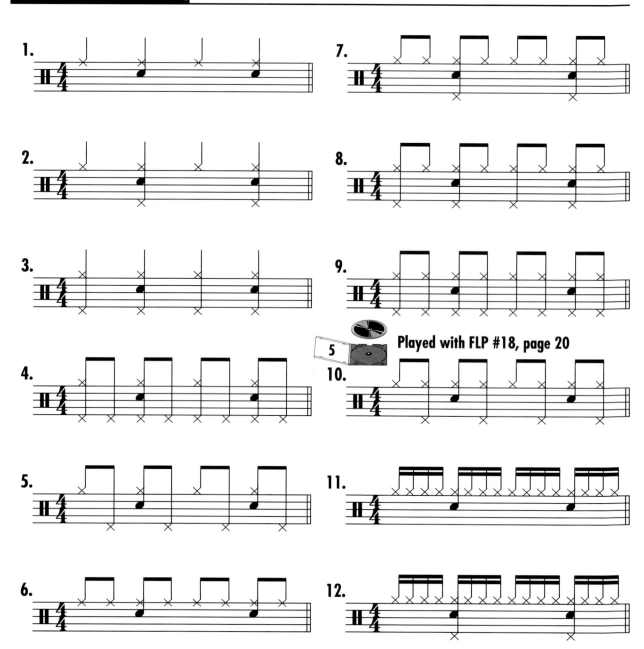

Played with FLP #18, page 20

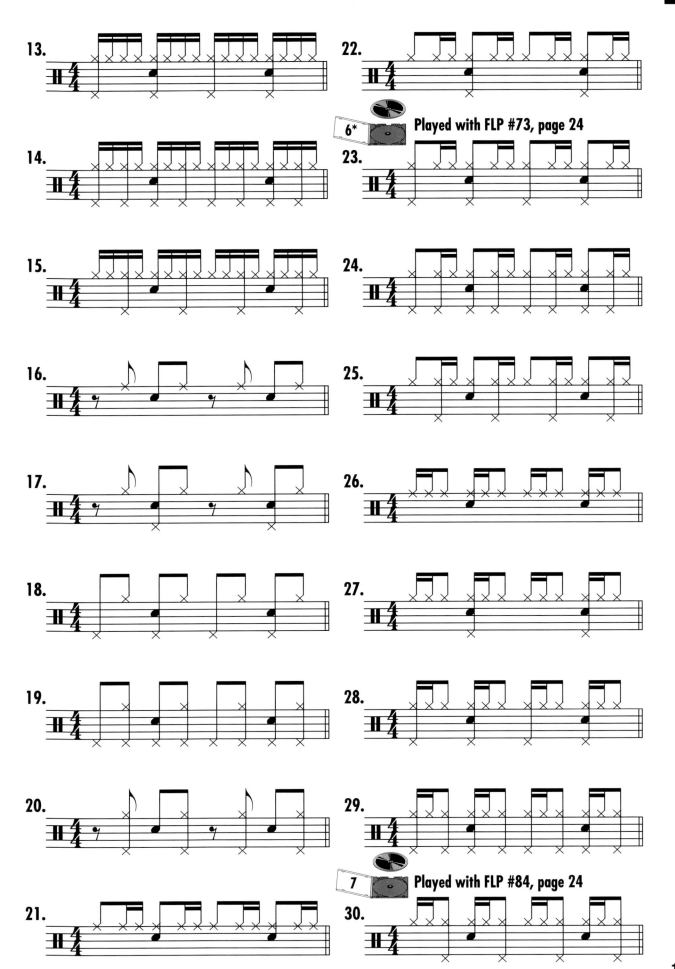

Played with FLP #73, page 24

Played with FLP #84, page 24

FLP (The Fourth Limb Patterns)

5 **Played with TLO #10, page 18**

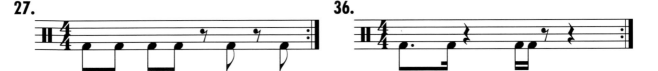

19.

20.

21.

22.

23.

24.

25.

26.

27.

28.

29.

30.

31.

32.

33.

34.

35.

36.

FLP (The Fourth Limb Patterns) *(continued)*

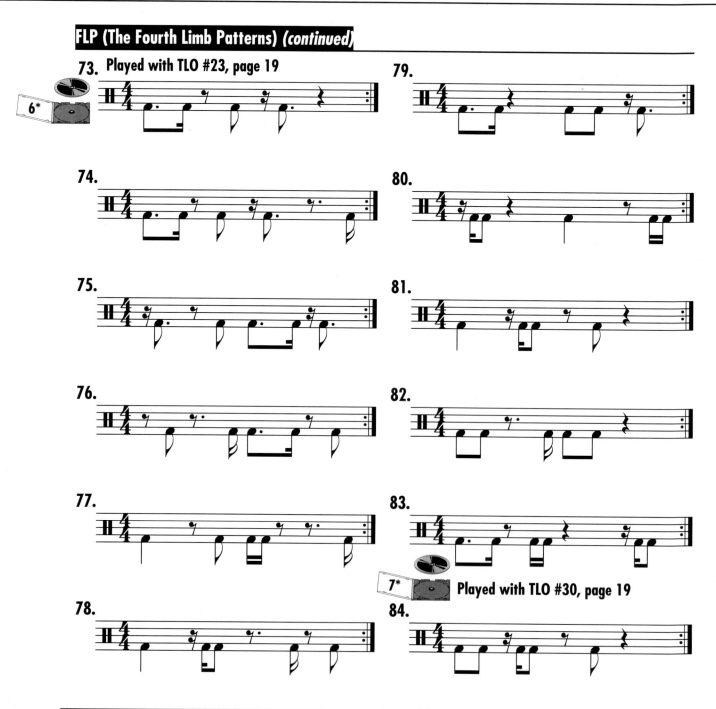

Advanced Groove Independence Exercises

Once you have mastered all the TLO and FLP combinations, practice the following four advanced concepts. Utilize the same FLPs, but change the feel of the grooves by altering the TLOs just a little bit.

1. Open Hi-Hat Ostinatos

Incorporate the following open and closed hi-hat patterns with each FLPs. This changes the feel of each groove drastically and creates a new approach to these independence exercises.

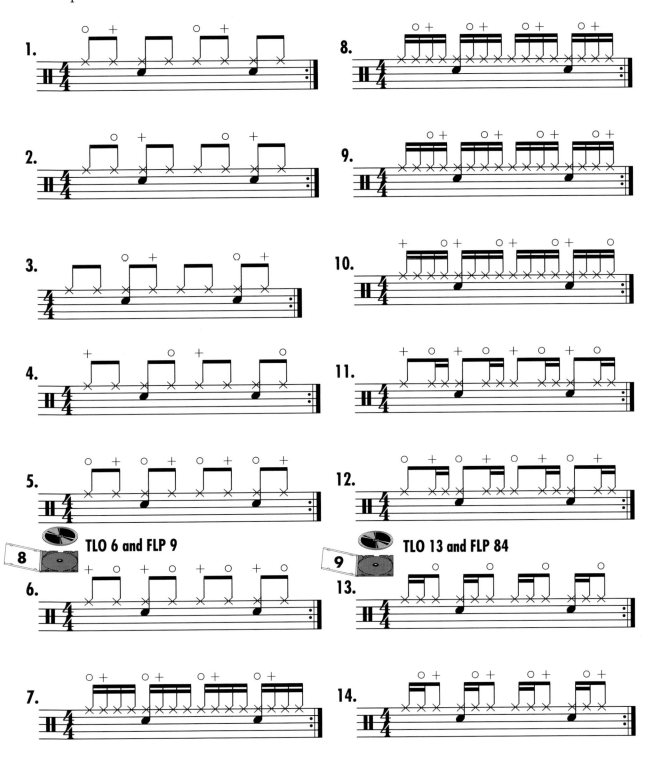

2. Left Foot Splashes

Now change the right-hand pattern to the ride cymbal and play the following hi-hat splash patterns with the left foot.

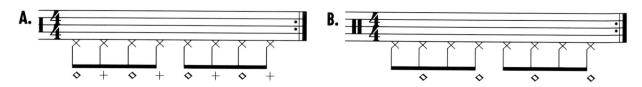

Here is an example of 1A with TLO #24 and FLP #2:

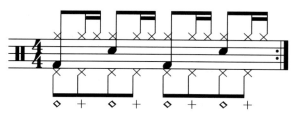

Here is an example of 1B with TLO #24 and FLP #2:

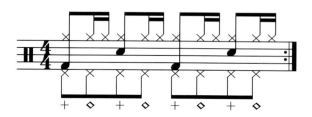

3. Half Time Feel

Change the left-hand limb (which up to this point have been on beats 2 and 4) so that it is playing on beat 3 only. This will change the groove to a half time feel. Here is an example of TLO #10 and FLP #11 using this concept:

4. Shuffle the Sixteenth-Note Ostinatos

Another advanced approach is to practice *shuffling the sixteenth notes* in all exercises containing sixteenth notes. Here is an example of TLO #11 and FLP #45 with the sixteenth notes shuffled:

Play as 16th-note funk shuffle.

Chapter 2

Subdivisions: Keeping It Even

Now that you have strengthened your groove independence skills, let's concentrate on lining up the limbs perfectly in time.

Against the Upbeat

In most cases, people practice with the click sounding on the downbeat of each beat. In these exercises, however, the click is replaced by a loop that emphasizes the upbeat. There are two reasons for doing this. The first is to help develop your subdivisions so that they are even and perfectly in time. The second is to develop concentration by not allowing the upbeat loop to disrupt your groove. Good concentration does not mean being stiff. Staying relaxed is important in making the time feel good.

On the CD, the two-beat count-off measure is the only measure in which you will hear the click accented on the downbeats. After that, the click is payed on the upbeats with the loop, and you will hear the emphasized upbeat loop. (The click will reappear periodically to guide you.) If you find yourself playing with the loop on the downbeat, you've lost your place and reversed the beat (turned the time around) so stop and try again.

For these exercises to be effective, you must practice them at various tempos. Three CD tracks with three tempos (slow, medium, and fast) have been provided for each subdivision you will practice. It is important for you to eventually experiment with other tempos than have been chosen for the CD. You can do this using the TNT 2 software.

Fred with "Mr. Solid" Steve Ferrone

1. Eighth-Note Subdivisions

These loops are based on eighth-note subdivisions (1-&-2-&-3-&-4-&). Once you begin to play, the loop will emphasis the "and" of each beat. Don't let this confuse you. Concentrate on keeping your groove and lining up all your limbs perfectly in time.

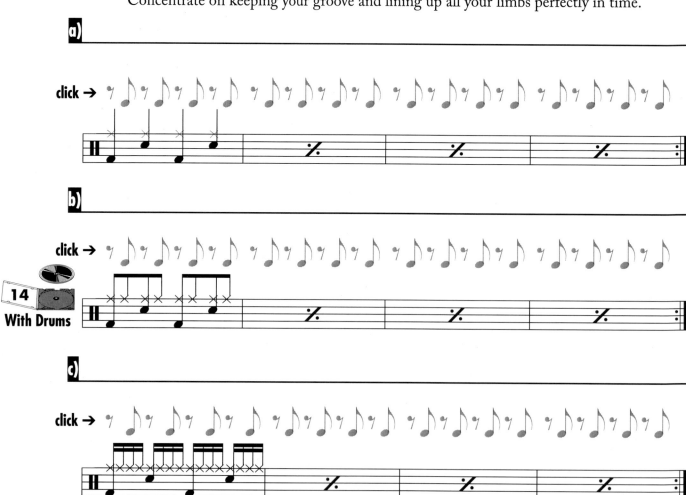

Slow Tempo Loop
67 BPM

Medium Tempo Loop
80 BPM

Fast Tempo Loop
125 BPM

2. Sixteenth-Note Subdivisions

These beats are based on sixteenth-note subdivisions (1-e-&-a 2-e-&-a 3-e-&-a 4-e-&-a).
Once you begin to play, the click will sound on the "e" and "a" of each beat. Again,
concentrate on keeping your groove and lining all your limbs perfectly in time.

Slow Tempo Loop
60 BPM

Medium Tempo Loop
84 BPM

Fast Tempo Loop
120 BPM

3. Eighth-Note Triplet Subdivisions

The following patterns are based on eighth-note triplet subdivisions:
(1 trip-let 2 trip-let 3 trip-let 4 trip-let).

a)

The click will sound on the downbeat of each beat of this exercise:

b)

22

With Drums

The click will sound on the second triplet (or the "trip") of each beat of this exercise:

c)

The click will sound on the third triplet (or the "let") of each beat in this exercise:

Click on the downbeat:	Click on the 2nd triplet:	Click on the last beat (let):
23 Slow Tempo 63 BPM	**26** Slow Tempo 60 BPM	**29** Slow Tempo 57 BPM
 **24** Medium Tempo 90 BPM	**27** Medium Tempo 76 BPM	 **30** Medium Tempo 94 BPM
25 Fast Tempo 125 BPM	**28** Fast Tempo 83 BPM	 **31** Fast Tempo 120 BPM

In most danceable grooves, beats 1, 2, and 4 are the most important. The consistency of these beats is paramount. The "Against the Upbeat" section of this chapter worked on lining up the subdivisions so that they were as precise as possible. That experience will assist you in this section, which is designed to help you place the quarter-note movement exactly where it should go. Similar to the previous exercises, these will also have slow, medium, and fast CD tracks to work with. When practicing these exercises, utilize the independence and subdivision skills you have already developed.

The "Big 1"

As the drummer, you have a responsibility to the band to provide a great feel and keep great time. Beat "1" is important because it is the beginning of each measure. The 1 of each measure is marking for the band exactly where the time begins. That is why it is known as the "Big 1." Play the following exercises, and try to hit the "1" consistently so that you do not hear the bass drum on the CD example, meaning you are in perfect sync with the recorded track and therefore keeping "perfect" time.

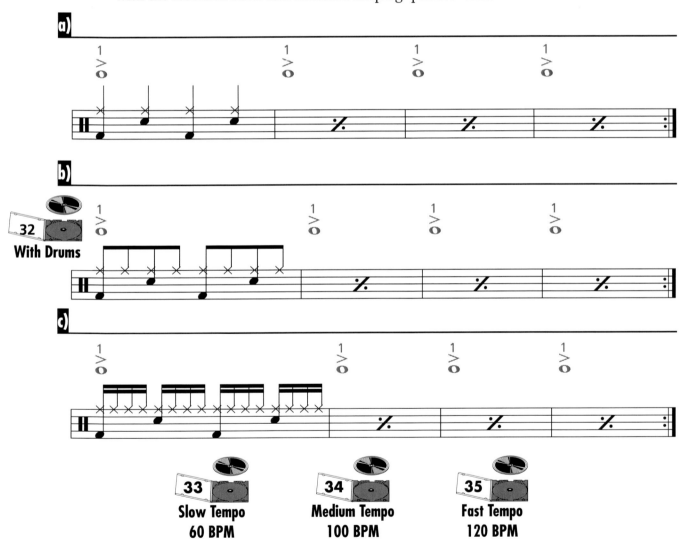

d)

2. The 2 & 4 Pocket

The drummer has a responsibility to the audience as well as to the band. Beats 2 and 4 are the beats that keep the audience dancing. They create the *pocket*. Without the pocket, there is no feel. In the styles of music we are working with in this study, it is the drummer's responsibility to the audience to provide this "pocket." Without this, the audience will not receive the full impact of the music and the performance.

In the recorded examples of each of these exercises, you will hear a hand-clap track on beats 2 and 4. The objective is to play so that you do not hear the hand-clap. That will mean you are playing beats 2 and 4 so consistently that you drown out, or "bury," the hand-clap. This exercise will immensely improve your pocket playing.

a)

b)

36
With Drums

c)

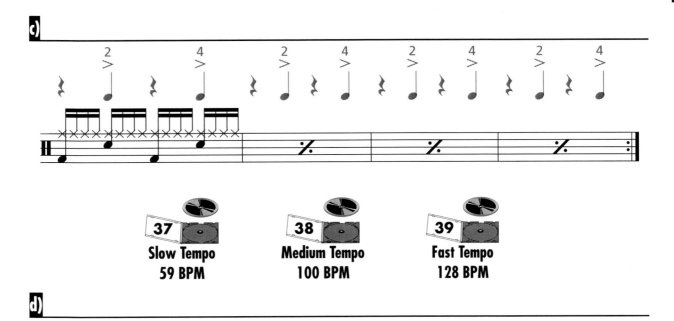

| **37** Slow Tempo 59 BPM | **38** Medium Tempo 100 BPM | **39** Fast Tempo 128 BPM |

d)

This exercise is based on eighth-note triplets:

Fred in his teaching studio

Play-Along 1: Two-4-One

40
With Drums

41
Minus Drums

In this first play-along chart, all the skills you have been working on up to this point will be utilized in a musical situation. The main objective is to concentrate on keeping all the subdivisions even, nailing the 1 and burying the 2 and 4 pocket. Make the song groove. That is the main objective.

You will hear the hand-claps and click throughout the piece, but the click sometimes sounds on the upbeat. Don't let this confuse you. Be confident in your time, and keep the subdivisions in mind at all times.

34

A Verse
Claps cont. on 2 & 4

A Solos Over Form   A B C A * (Be aware of the click and the music moving to the upbeats.)

B

C   Bridge

Bridge Cont.

Breakdown
Claps
C

Outro   * (The click will move from downbeats to upbeats.)

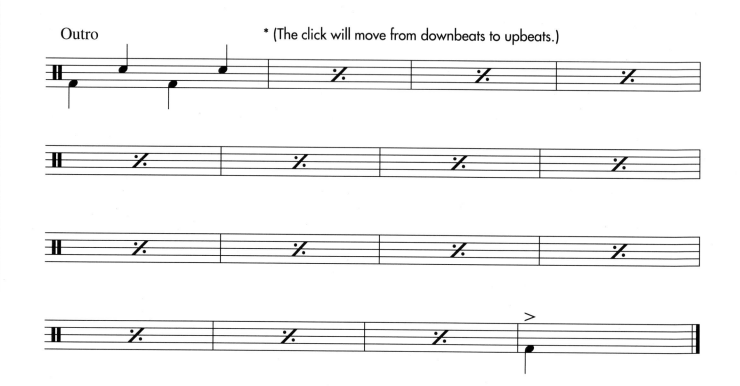

Fred with the great Louie Bellson

Chapter 3

Playing the Space

Whenever you practice (and sometimes when you perform), it is very important to use a metronome or click of some kind. It is equally important, however, not to become dependent on the click. In other words, the click should be used to help develop a better internal clock or sense of time so you will be just as solid when there is no click. The exercises in this chapter deal primarily with space and how to play with it consistently—without a click.

Short Periods of Space

Each exercise is deliberately designed with missing "click" beats. Sometimes 1, 2, 3, or 4 beats at a time are left with no click or sequence—just blank space. The objective of these exercises is to play through the space in perfect time so that when the click comes back, you are still in time. During these moments of space, you will not hear the click, so you won't be dependent on an outside clock—only your internal clock. It's a good idea to record yourself while playing these exercises. Hearing yourself recorded will allow you to analyze your playing. You'll get a good sense of your progress with these exercises and concepts.

Each exercise has three CD tracks (slow, medium, and fast) for each space movement. The following beats are suggested starting points for the exercises in all the tempos that are marked "time played here." You should also practice these exercises with other grooves.

Quarter-Note Groove

Eighth-Note Groove

Sixteenth-Note Groove

Preparation Exercise

To get a solid understanding, practice each exercise by clapping and vocalizing the downbeats out loud only—do not play anything. Once you feel that you can clap and count the beats out loud through the space, continue with playing the exercises.

1. Quarter-Note Space

Practice each of these exercises with each of the four grooves.

 a)

This exercise contains one beat of space on the fourth beat of the fourth measure.

Beat 4
space

Use these tracks for practicing the One-Beat Fills.

Slow Tempo
62 BPM

Medium Tempo
95 BPM

Fast Tempo
130 BPM

 b)

This exercise contains one beat of space on the third beat of the fourth measure.

Beat 3
space

Slow Tempo
59 BPM

Medium Tempo
87 BPM

Fast Tempo
135 BPM

c)

This exercise contains one beat of space on the second beat of the fourth measure.

48	**49**	**50**
Slow Tempo	Medium Tempo	Fast Tempo
67 BPM	102 BPM	137 BPM

d)

This exercise contains one beat of space on the first beat of the fourth measure.

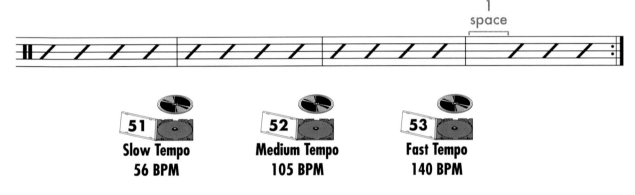

51	**52**	**53**
Slow Tempo	Medium Tempo	Fast Tempo
56 BPM	105 BPM	140 BPM

2. Half-Note Space

These exercises contain two beats of space. Practice each of them with the same four grooves.

a)

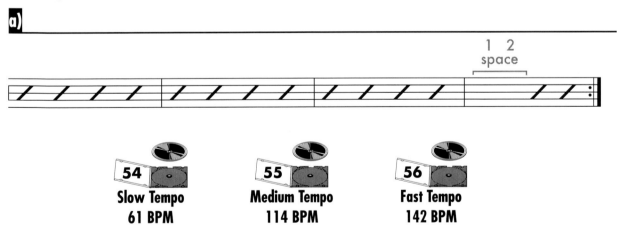

54	**55**	**56**
Slow Tempo	Medium Tempo	Fast Tempo
61 BPM	114 BPM	142 BPM

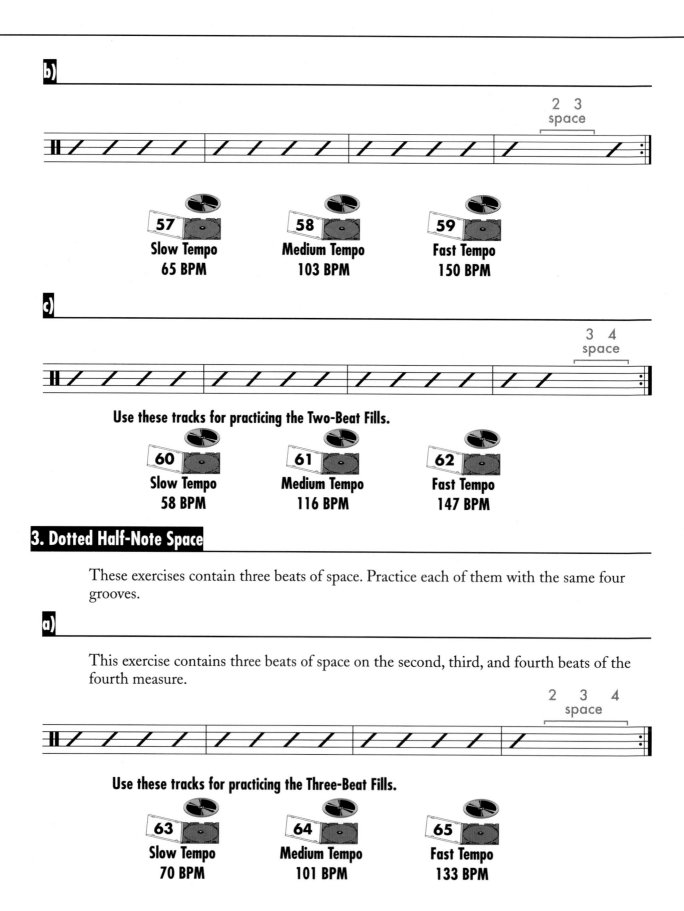

b)

2 3
space

| 57 | 58 | 59 |
Slow Tempo | Medium Tempo | Fast Tempo
65 BPM | 103 BPM | 150 BPM

c)

3 4
space

Use these tracks for practicing the Two-Beat Fills.

| 60 | 61 | 62 |
Slow Tempo | Medium Tempo | Fast Tempo
58 BPM | 116 BPM | 147 BPM

3. Dotted Half-Note Space

These exercises contain three beats of space. Practice each of them with the same four grooves.

a)

This exercise contains three beats of space on the second, third, and fourth beats of the fourth measure.

2 3 4
space

Use these tracks for practicing the Three-Beat Fills.

| 63 | 64 | 65 |
Slow Tempo | Medium Tempo | Fast Tempo
70 BPM | 101 BPM | 133 BPM

b)

This exercise contains three beats of space on the first, second, and third beats of the fourth measure.

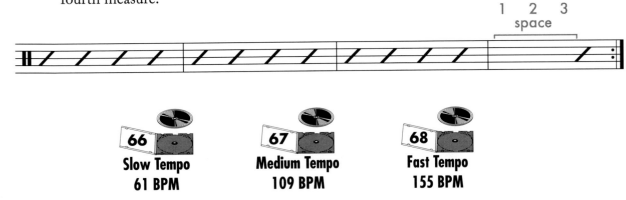

66
Slow Tempo
61 BPM

67
Medium Tempo
109 BPM

68
Fast Tempo
155 BPM

4. Whole-Note Space

This exercise contains four beats of space in the fourth measure. Continue using the suggested patterns.

Use these tracks for practicing the Four-Beat Fills.

69
Slow Tempo
75 BPM

70
Medium Tempo
85 BPM

71
Fast Tempo
153 BPM

Long Periods of Space

With the exception of having longer periods of space, these exercises are identical to those in the "Short Periods of Space" section. This is a fun way to master your control of playing the space. Continue using the suggested patterns.

1. Two Bars of Space

This exercise contains eight beats of space in measures 3 and 4.

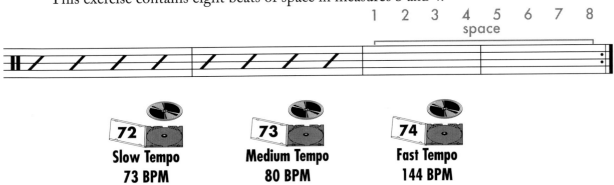

72
Slow Tempo
73 BPM

73
Medium Tempo
80 BPM

74
Fast Tempo
144 BPM

2. Four Bars of Space

This exercise is an eight-bar phrase. It contains 16 beats of space in measures 5, 6, 7, and 8.

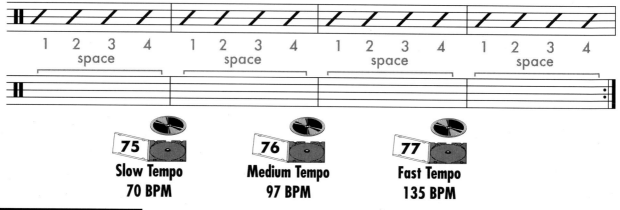

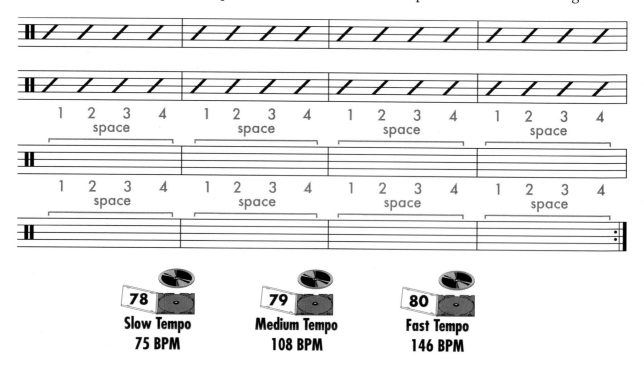		

75 Slow Tempo 70 BPM   **76** Medium Tempo 97 BPM   **77** Fast Tempo 135 BPM

3. Eight Bars of Space

This exercise is a 16-bar phrase. It contains 32 beats of space in measures 9 through 16.

78 Slow Tempo 75 BPM   **79** Medium Tempo 108 BPM   **80** Fast Tempo 146 BPM

Middle Changes

Up to this point in the book, you have worked on getting your subdivisions lined up, even, and consistent. Having this skill is important, especially with what you are going to practice now—Middle Changes.

In most musical situations, it is very common to have a change in the subdivision of the groove, especially when going from one section of the song to another, such as from verse to chorus. The exercises in this section are designed to help you develop the ability to change subdivisions in mid-play, without losing your groove.

In these exercises, the subdivision always changes in the hi-hat part. Each groove has a steady bass drum groove on beats 1 and 3 and the snare drum on 2 and 4. All of the exercises in this section are written as four-bar phrases with two different subdivisions indicated in the hi-hat part. The first and third measures are based in one subdivision, while the second and fourth measures are based in another. To ensure you are concentrating (and utilizing your Fifth Limb), the click disappears in the second and fourth measures. This means you have to change the subdivision (without a click), and then go back to the original subdivision (with the click).

Use CD Tracks 81–83 for all of these exercises. Once you get the hang of these exercises, go back and utilize the audio tracks in the "Long Periods of Space" section. This will give you the opportunity to practice four- and eight bar soloing as well, but first make sure you have mastered playing the time in the space.

81	**82**	**83**
Slow Tempo	Medium Tempo	Fast Tempo
60 BPM	80 BPM	127 BPM

1. Quarter Changes

a) to Eighths

b) to Sixteenths

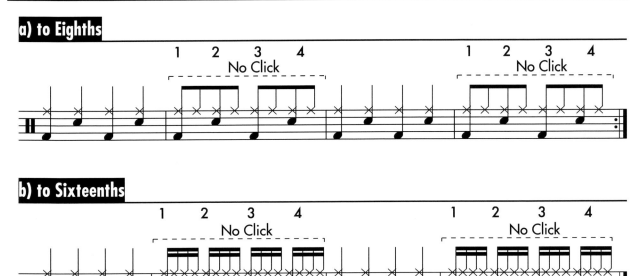

c) to Eighth-Note Triplets

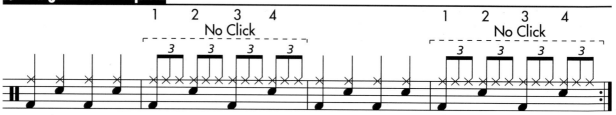

Optional Groove

d) to Triplet Shuffle

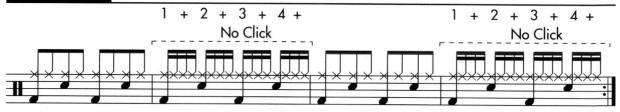

2. Eighth-Note Changes

a) to Quarters

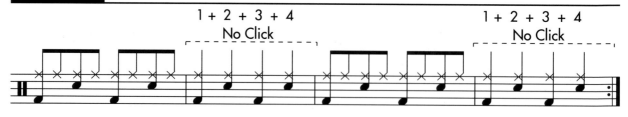

b) to Sixteenths

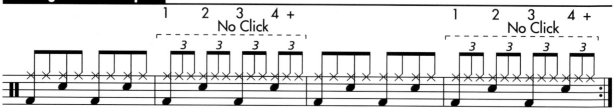

c) to Eighth-Note Triplets

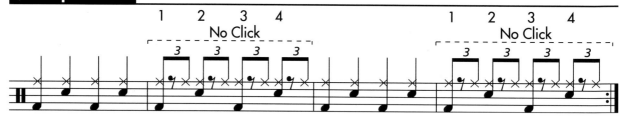

Optional Groove

d) to Triplet Shuffle

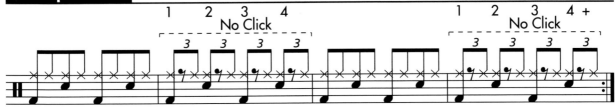

3. Sixteenth-Note Changes

a) to Quarters

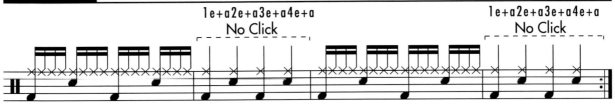

b) to Eighths

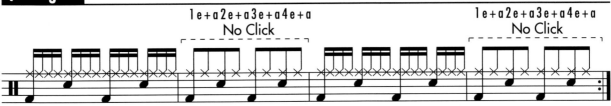

c) to Eighth-Note Triplets

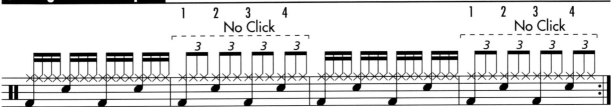

Optional Groove

d) to Triplet Shuffle

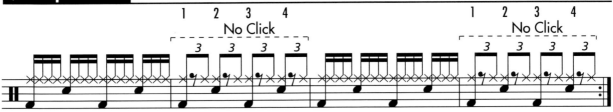

4. Triplet Note Changes

a) to Quarters

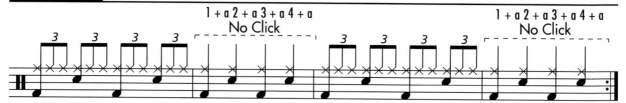

b) to Eighths

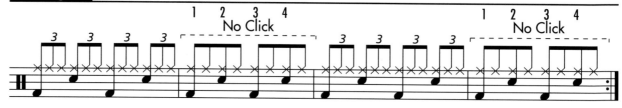

c) to Sixteenths

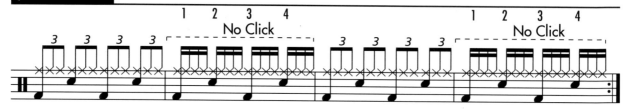

Optional Groove

d) to Triplet Shuffle

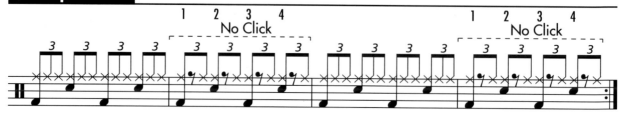

46

Middle Changes on the Upbeats

Now that you have the concept of Middle Changes mastered, use each of the same changes (quarter, eighth, sixteenth, and eighth-note triplets) in conjunction with the following subdivision upbeats. Continue using CD Tracks 81–83 when working with the following exercises.

1. To Eighth-Note Upbeats

2. To Eighth-Note Upbeats (e)

3. To Eighth-Note Upbeats (a)

4. To Eighth-Note Upbeats (e, a)

5. To Eighth-Note Upbeats (e, &)

6. To Eighth-Note Upbeats (&, a)

7. To Eighth-Note Triplet Upbeats (pull)

8. To Eighth-Note Triplet Upbeats (let)

9. To Eighth-Note Triplet Upbeats (pull, let)

Advanced Middle Changes Exercises

A great way to improve your "mid-play" subdivision performance and ability around the kit is to move the hi-hat parts around. In other words, play the hi-hat "subdivision" part randomly around the kit (toms, cymbals, etc.) on the second and fourth measures. You can practice this on all the Middle Changes exercises and, when you really begin to master it, you can get creative by combining and interchanging the various subdivisions.

Count-Offs

A common problem with many musicians is that their tempo differs from the given count-off. In other words, the count-off is at one tempo while the tune ends up slower or faster and ultimately "grooveless." It sometimes takes at least four measures before the time settles into a good groove. These exercises are designed to help you grab the countoff tempo and maintain it throughout the complete tune—start to finish. Let's examine four of the most common count-offs: two-bar, one-bar, two-beat, and one-beat.

In each exercise you, will be given the count-off. Start playing the suggested pattern or a groove of your own choosing. Either a snare drum on beats 2 and 4 or bass drum on beats 1 and 3 will sound out randomly. If your time remains consistent with the count off given, the snare and bass drum hits will line up with yours. This is very tricky but a lot of fun. Each example will be in three different tempos: fast, medium, and slow.

Play this beat with all the examples:

1. Two-Bar Count-Offs

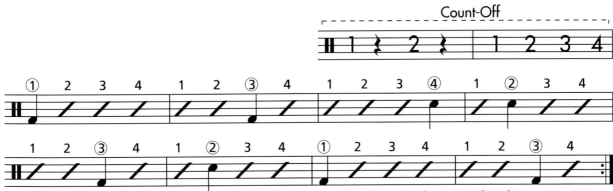

For loops 85 and 86 this exercise continues for eight more bars with various reference points (the quarter notes within each bar). You must be sure that you are in sync with each of these beats.

84
Slow Tempo
62 BPM

85
Medium Tempo
84 BPM

86
Fast Tempo
129 BPM

2. One-Bar Count-Offs

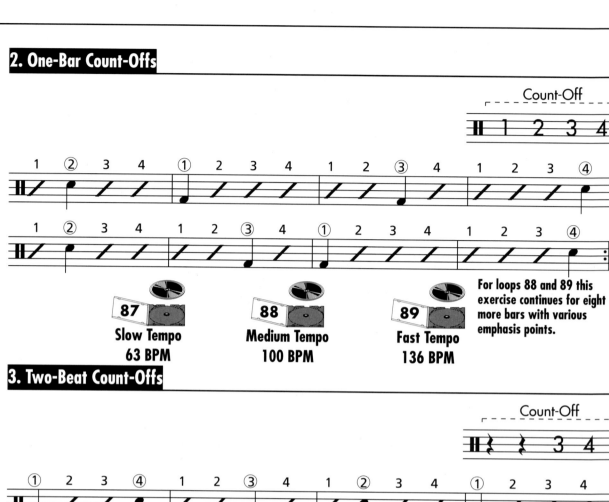

For loops 88 and 89 this exercise continues for eight more bars with various emphasis points.

87 Slow Tempo 63 BPM

88 Medium Tempo 100 BPM

89 Fast Tempo 136 BPM

3. Two-Beat Count-Offs

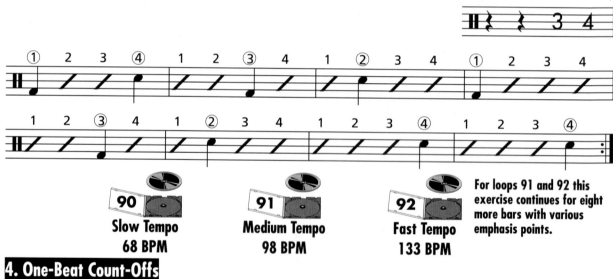

For loops 91 and 92 this exercise continues for eight more bars with various emphasis points.

90 Slow Tempo 68 BPM

91 Medium Tempo 98 BPM

92 Fast Tempo 133 BPM

4. One-Beat Count-Offs

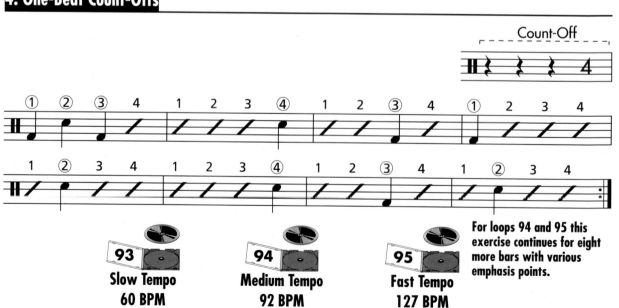

For loops 94 and 95 this exercise continues for eight more bars with various emphasis points.

93 Slow Tempo 60 BPM

94 Medium Tempo 92 BPM

95 Fast Tempo 127 BPM

Fred with Harvey Mason and John Blackwell

Fred demonstrates the pocket during a clinic

Play-Along 2: Space Boogie

This play-along mixes all of the various space examples into one piece. Some of the space examples come after each other, creating a large amount of space, so be sure to concentrate. In addition, there are mid-play subdivision changes.

96 With Drums   **97** Minus Drums

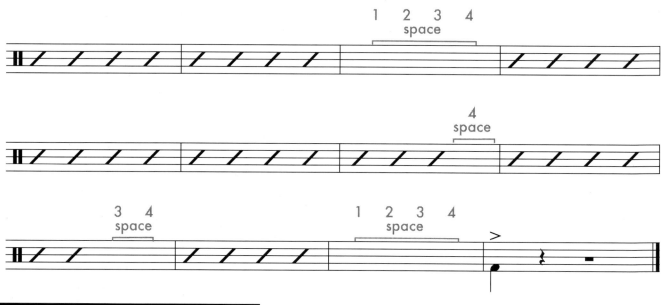

Fred with his Extreme Isolation headphones laying down the song "Emotions"

Chapter 4

The Drum Fill Workout

Drum fills can be one of the most challenging areas of execution. Drummers often speed up or slow down before or after playing a drum fill. Others seem to rush during the end of a phrase—especially when going into a new section.

Through the years of rock and R&B drumming, certain fills have become referred to as the "money fills." These fills have been used on various hit records throughout the years. Though they may sound and look simple when written, they are not always simple to execute in "perfect" time.

There are a total of 40 fills: ten one-beat fills, ten two-beat fills, ten three-beat fills, and ten four-beat fills. Using the MP3 tracks from Disc 1, practice the fills by playing each within a four-bar phrase: three bars of time, with the fourth bar containing the fill. Play your hi-hat foot on either 2 and 4 or quarter notes during your fill to help you keep the time. This, in addition to your Fifth Limb, will help keep the subdivisions even.

1. One-Beat Fills

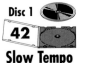

| Disc 1 **42** Slow Tempo | Disc 1 **43** Medium Tempo | Disc 1 **44** Fast Tempo |

1.

2.

3.

2. Two-Beat Fills

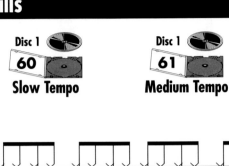

Disc 1 **60** **Slow Tempo** **Disc 1** **61** **Medium Tempo** **Disc 1** **62** **Fast Tempo**

1.

2.

3.

4.

5.

6.

7.

57

8.

9.

10.

3. Three-Beat Fills

Disc 1 **63** Slow Tempo

Disc 1 **64** Medium Tempo

Disc 1 **65** Fast Tempo

1.

2.

3.

4.

4. Four-Beat Fills

 Disc 1 **69** **Slow Tempo**   **Disc 1** **70** **Medium Tempo**   **Disc 1** **71** **Fast Tempo**

1.

2.

3.

4.

5.

6.

7.

8.

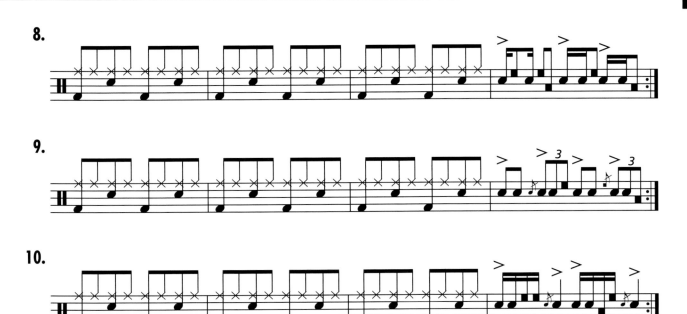

9.

10.

Advanced Exercises

Once you get used to practicing the fills on the fourth bar of each phrase, go back to Chapter 3: "Playing the Space," and practice by filling the provided space in each "Short Periods of Space" exercise with the fills. These spaces come and go on various beats within the measures. It may not be very musical, but it is good way to test your fill capability.

Fred demonstrating "Playing the Space" during a clinic performance

Play-Along 3: How Do You Fill?

98
With Drums

99
Medium Tempo

Now that you feel comfortable playing each fill with the hi-hat foot, practice utilizing them within a musical situation. The end of each musical section will contain dead space, marked "fill." Practice playing your fill in these spots and concentrate on coming back out on the "1."

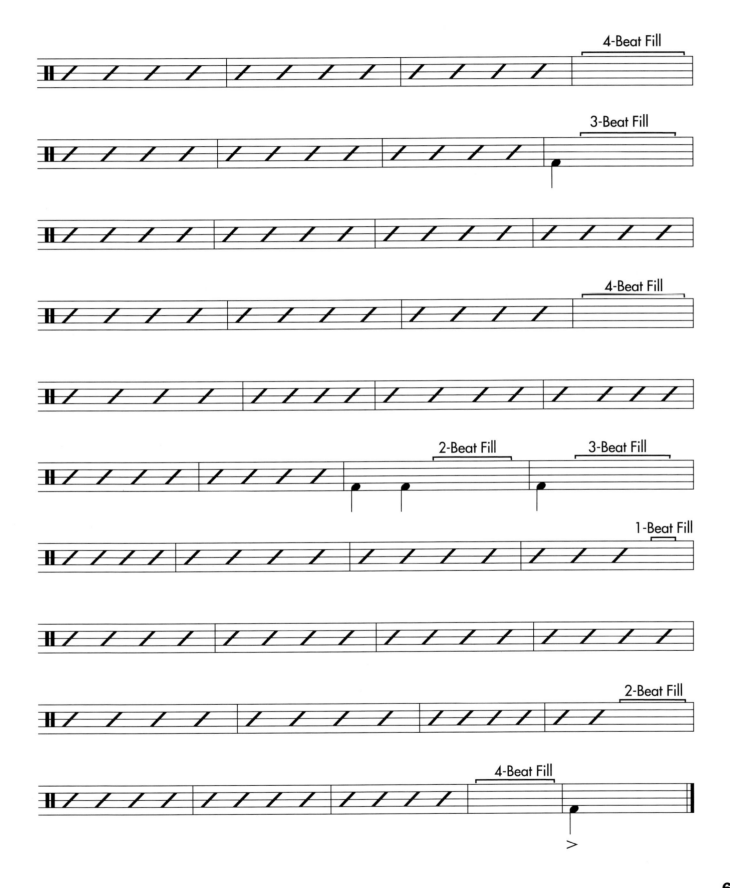

Fred with his teacher and mentor Joe Porcaro

Fred with Dennis Chambers

Chapter 5

Playing the Hits

Drummers are often required to play fills or accents in unison with other musicians. This is sometimes called "playing the hits" or "ensemble" figures. This chapter will help you with playing these hits in a practice forum, so that when you play with a band, you will be able to do so. Playing together as a band is critical to playing ensemble figures. If any of the hits are not together, a disruption in the groove will occur.

Hits and Accents

In these exercises you will play your hits with a horn section. The key is to play the horn hits that are given at the end of each four-bar phrase while maintaining the groove in good time. The groove you play in the first three bars is up to you—as long as it grooves with the loop. Since there is limited space on the CD, there is only one medium tempo for each exercise. Practice each exercise in a three-step manner:

Preparation Exercise #1

Practice each exercise by vocalizing the downbeats (fifth limb) and clapping the hits and accents.

Preparation Exercise #2

Now play the hits and accents on the snare drum instead of clapping.

Preparation Exercise #3

Once you are comfortable with the figures, add the crash cymbal. To do this, double the hits and accents by hitting the snare drum with one hand and hitting a crash cymbal with the other, or by using the bass drum to reinforce the crash cymbal. Remember to vocalize your fifth limb.

Hits and Accents Exercises

The following exercises (1–48) are part of one continuous loop which is to be played as one long sequence. In order to make an individual loop, you will need to have access to programs such as Garage Band, Pro Tools, Ableton Live, etc. A count-off is only provided for exercise 1.

1.   Disc 2   **1**

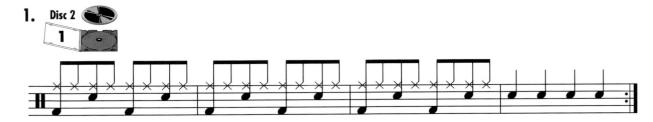

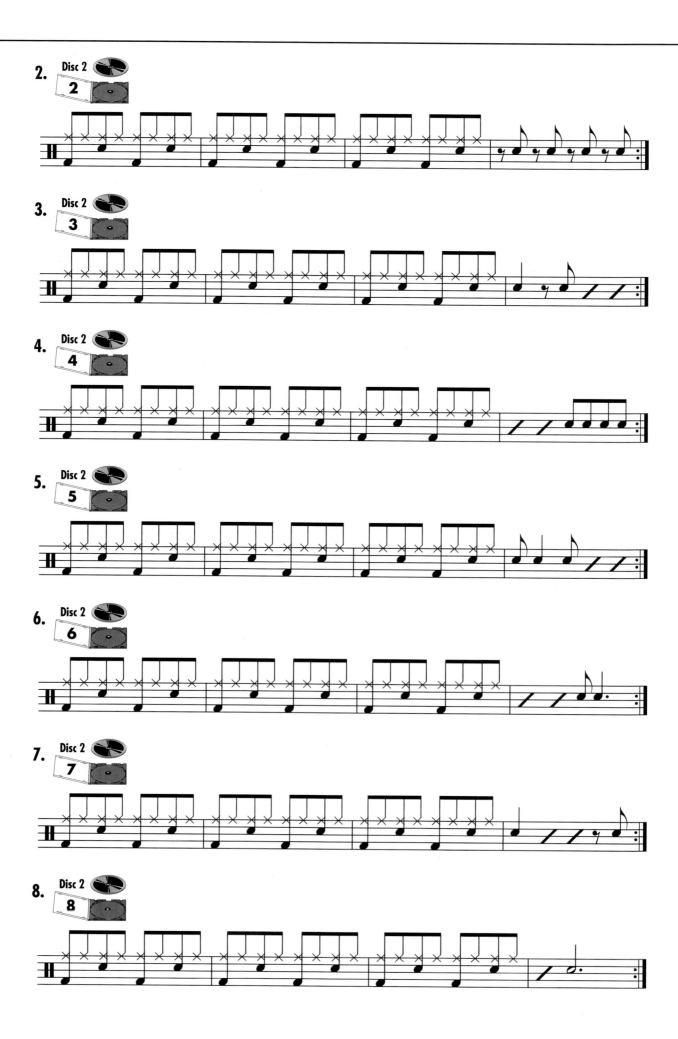

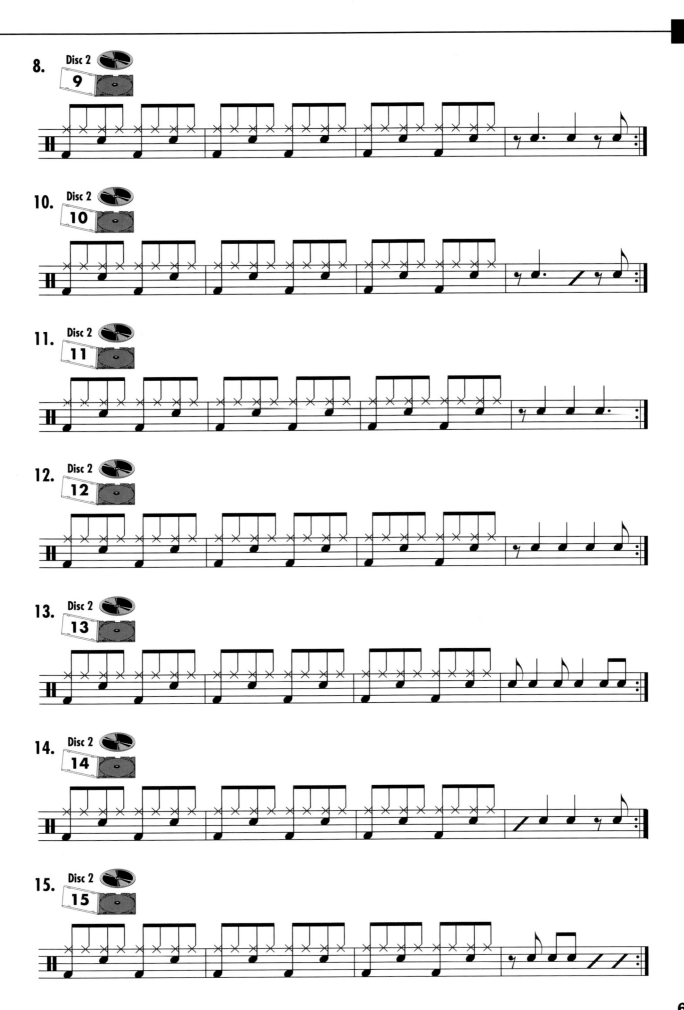

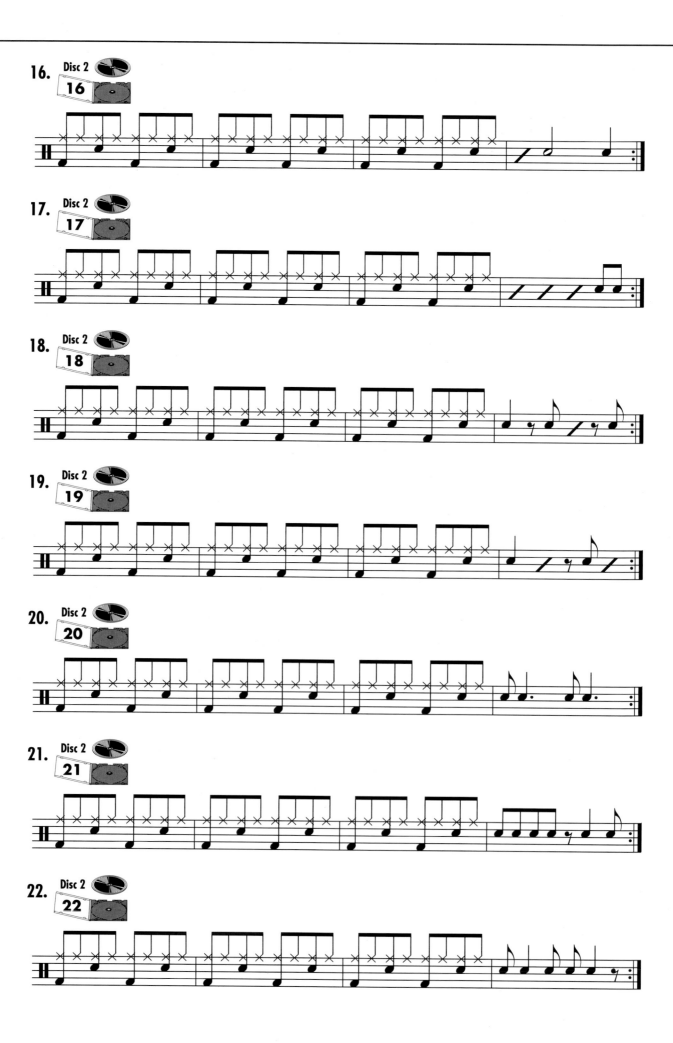

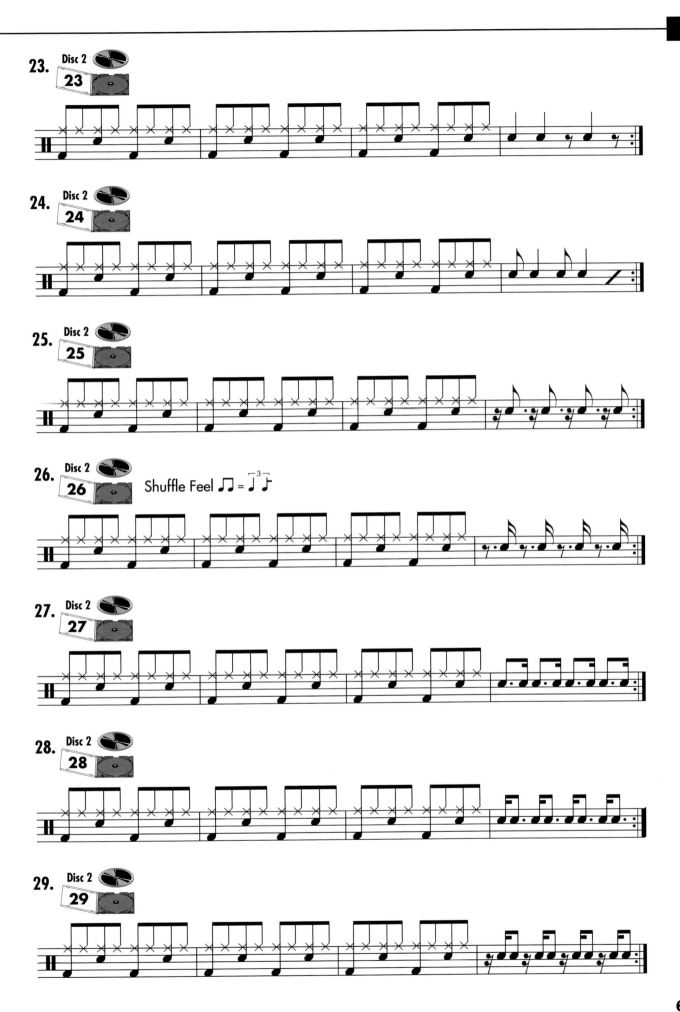

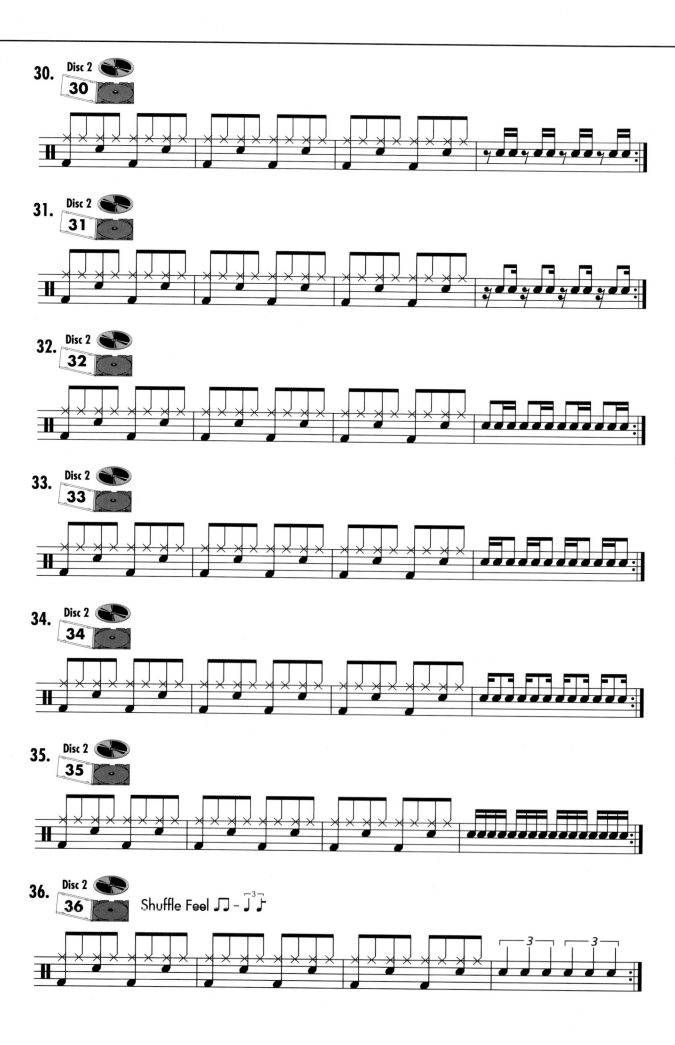

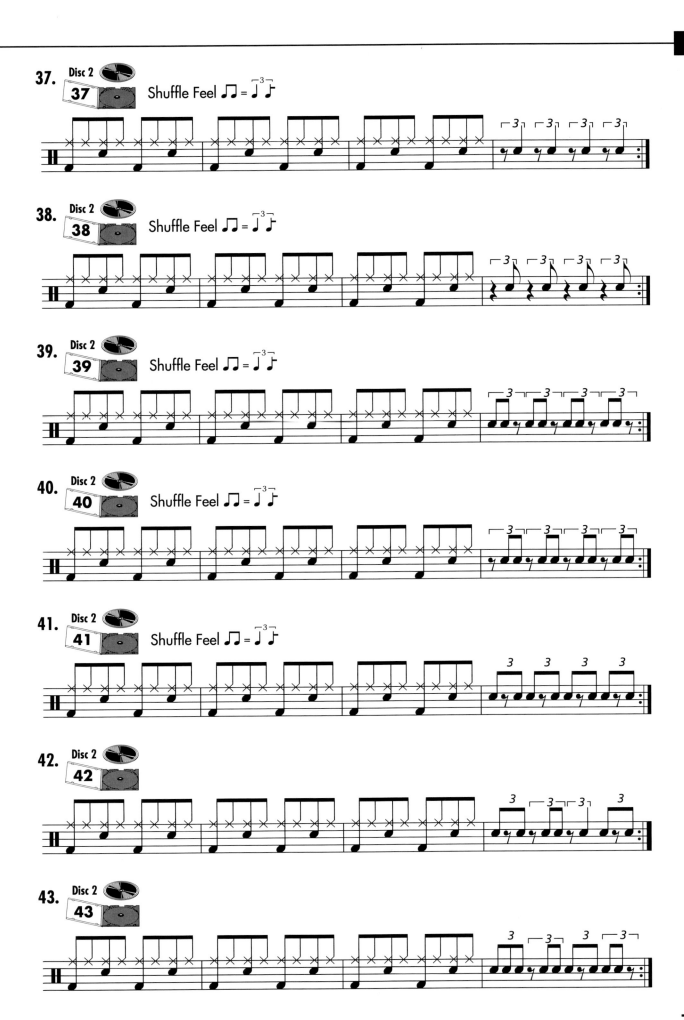

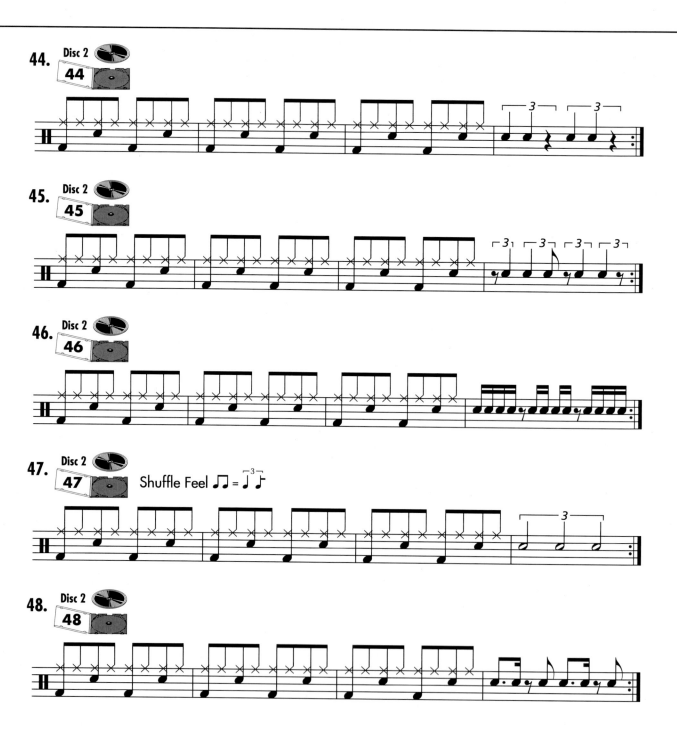

44. Disc 2 | 44

45. Disc 2 | 45

46. Disc 2 | 46

47. Disc 2 | 47

Shuffle Feel

48. Disc 2 | 48

Play-Along 4: Just Hit Me

This chart was written specifically for you to practice playing time and horn hits (section figures) only, with no set-ups or fills. Playing this correctly is the most fundamental concept and technique that you must master in order to play meaningful setups and fills around these figures.

Piano Solo

Set-Ups

Once you have mastered accenting the hits, practice setting each one up with a fill. "Setting up" a hit is when you play a fill just prior to the accents of the hits. In these exercises, the fill will begin either on beat 3 or 4 of bar 3—just prior to the hits in bar 4. Three examples of this are demonstrated on the CD.

1. Disc 2 **51**

2.

3.

4.

5. Disc 2 **52**

6.

7.

8.

9.

10.

11.

12.

13.

14.

15.

16.

17.

18.

Play-Along 5: Hitsville

Now practice these concepts within an actual chart. Read down the chart and play the hits as written within the music. Once you play down the chart a few times, you will become more familiar and comfortable with it. At that point, you should begin practicing the set-ups for each hit.

Disc 2 — **53** — **With Drums**

Disc 2 — **54** — **Minus Drums**

There is a 6-beat count-off for this chart: 4 bars of count-off and the first two beats of the pick-up bar.

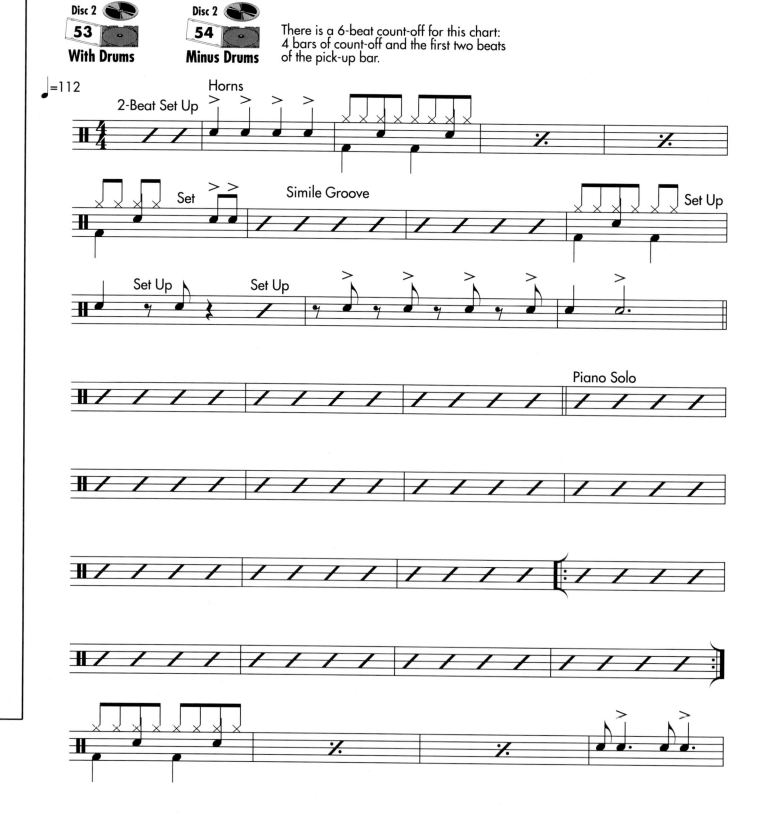

Fred during a clinic performance

Chapter 6

Time Movement and Feel

The time movement of a song is based on the emotional statement that the composer is trying to achieve. Put simply, the groove will determine the emotion of the song. The major concentration of this book, up to this point, has been on the technical abilities of improving time. However, being a good musician is more than being technically efficient. Ultimately, time movement is about feel and should not be considered as a mere technical endeavor.

The most common time movements, or "feels," are described as "playing on top," "playing behind," and "playing in the middle" of the beat. Understanding how to hear and feel the difference between these three concepts will make you a better drummer and a better musician. Remember to apply an emotional approach to these exercises rather than only a technical one.

A great way to capture the feel of a specific time movement is to use the Fifth Limb technique. Your voice can play an important part in capturing the appropriate groove. Try singing the most fundamental subdivision of each groove when practicing.

In these exercises, you will hear a cross-stick on the CD with the appropriate time feel. The cross-stick appears on beats 2 and 4 and is there to help you realize the proper time feel. Play along and try to match the cross-stick.

Try recording yourself practicing these exercises. Listening to yourself is one of the best ways to zone in on problem areas.

The following beat will be used for each of these exercises:

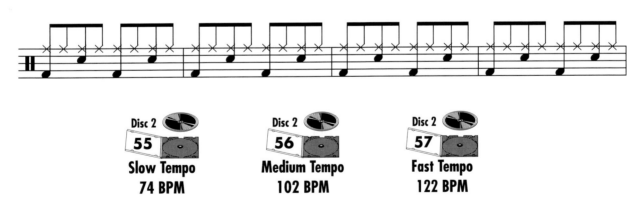

Disc 2	Disc 2	Disc 2
55	**56**	**57**
Slow Tempo	**Medium Tempo**	**Fast Tempo**
74 BPM	**102 BPM**	**122 BPM**

Playing on Top of the Beat

Playing "on top" of the beat gives the sense of pushing ever so slightly. Your playing pushes the band forward but does not rush. This type of time movement is used most often to convey an uplifting, excited, or happy mood.

Playing in the Middle of the Beat

Playing "in the middle" of the beat gives a balanced sense to the groove. Your playing keeps the band dead on. This type of time movement is used most often to convey a general in-the-middle feeling.

Disc 2	Disc 2	Disc 2
58	**59**	**60**
Slow Tempo	**Medium Tempo**	**Fast Tempo**
74 BPM	**102 BPM**	**122 BPM**

Playing Behind the Beat

Playing "behind" the beat gives a laid-back feel. Your playing pulls the band back without dragging. This type of time movement is used most often to provoke a bluesy, lazy, or sad mood. It is also very often used to convey a down-and-dirty kind of feeling.

Disc 2	Disc 2	Disc 2
61	**62**	**63**
Slow Tempo	**Medium Tempo**	**Fast Tempo**
74 BPM	**102 BPM**	**122 BPM**

Fred with the Emotions

Fred with Doane Perry

Greg Moore, Fred, and Paul Jackson, Jr.

Play-Along 6: Emotions

Disc 2
64
With Drums

Disc 2
65
Minus Drums

Now play along with this chart and try to change the emotion of the song. Practice playing the song with the three feels: behind, ahead, and in the middle of the beat. By doing this, you will realize the importance of your role as a drummer to the feel of a piece of music. You have the ability to change the whole emotion of a piece.

The cross-stick is provided in the audio tracks to assist you with playing the correct feel.

84

Fred with Wayne Blanchard of Sabian Cymbals

Fred with Bill Zildjian and Bobby Boos of Sabian Cymbals

Fred helping a student find the time

Fred presenting his time and groove concepts

Chapter 7

The "Time Maze"

The "Time Maze" is a composition that incorporates each exercise you have studied in the book and tests your mastery of each topic. The chart gives you a guideline to follow so you will know what is coming up. If you have truly mastered time, then you will get to the end of the chart in one piece. This is a fun way to assess your new time awareness.

Disc 2

Tracks 66-74

The remaining CD tracks are a few examples of my friends playing the "Time Maze," each in his own way. Keep in mind that these are professionals who have been playing for a long time and have mastered the various aspects of time playing. I hope you are inspired by these tracks. It is important to hear what is possible if you spend time working on your "time." Enjoy!

CD 2 Track 66 The "Time Maze"-Fred Dinkins With Drums

CD 2 Track 67 The "Time Maze"-Fred Dinkins Minus Drums

CD 2 Track 68 The "Time Maze"-ARTIST: Harvey Mason

CD 2 Track 69 The "Time Maze"-ARTIST: Ricky Lawson

CD 2 Track 70 The "Time Maze"-ARTIST: Curt Bisquera

CD 2 Track 71 The "Time Maze"-ARTIST: Land Richards

CD 2 Track 72 The "Time Maze"-ARTIST: Doane Perry

CD 2 Track 73 The "Time Maze"-ARTIST: Gerry Brown

CD 2 Track 74 The "Time Maze"-ARTIST: Dennis Chambers

Play-Along 7: The "Time Maze"

3/4 over 4/4 continued

Bridge   1/2 x Feel (Behind the Beat)

Melody   The Big One Back to the Middle of the Beat

Fred performing the "Time Maze" during a clinic presentation

Chapter 8

Grooving in 3/4

To truly master time, it is important to practice in all tempos and in every time signature. Various tempos are included in this book, but the limited space on the CDs only allows the recording of a small number of tempo variations. Regarding time signatures, all of the previous exercises are written in 4/4. You should use a drum machine or sequencer and program various exercises in all tempos and time signatures.

Here are a few TLOs and FLPs in 3/4 time to get you started.

3/4 TLOs

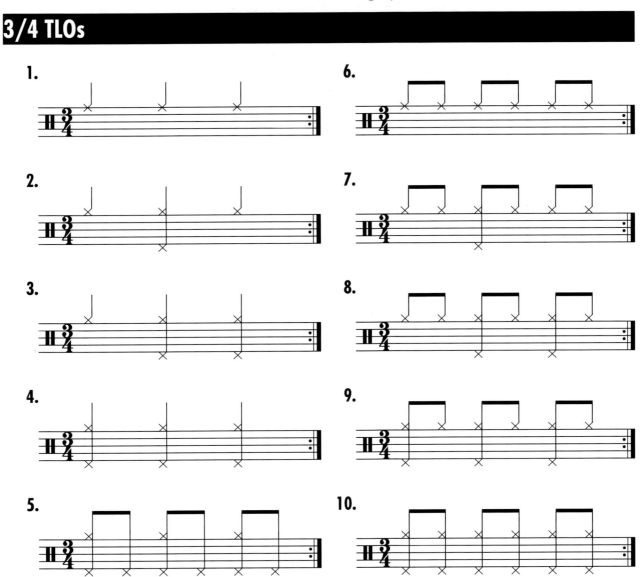

3/4 TLOs (continued)

11.

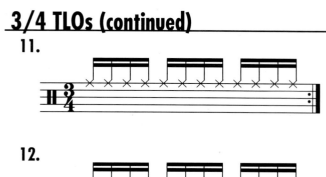

12.

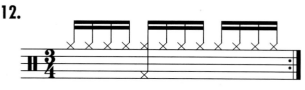

13.

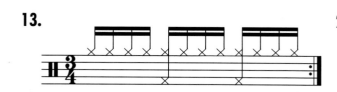

14.

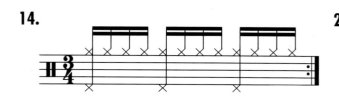

15.

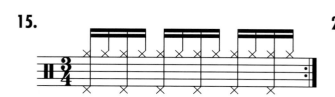

16.

17.

18.

19.

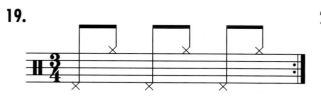

20.

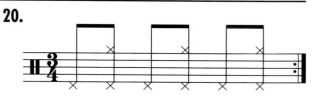

21.

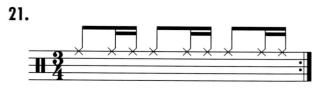

22.

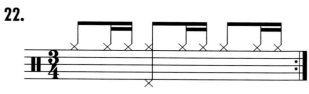

23.

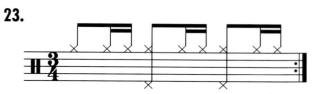

24.

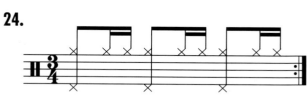

25.

26.

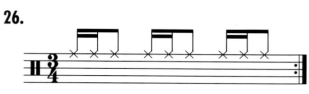

27.

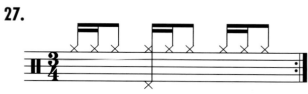

28.

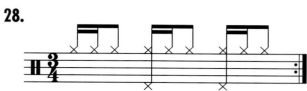

3/4 TLOs (continued)

29.

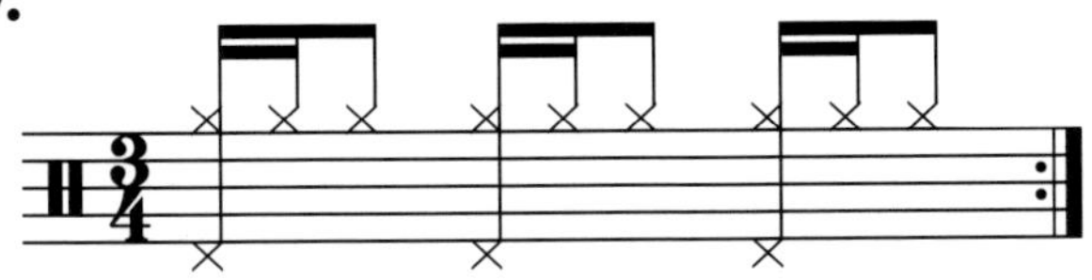

30.

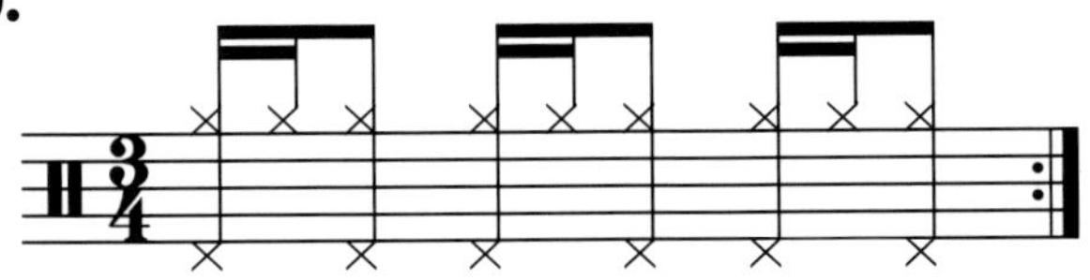

31.

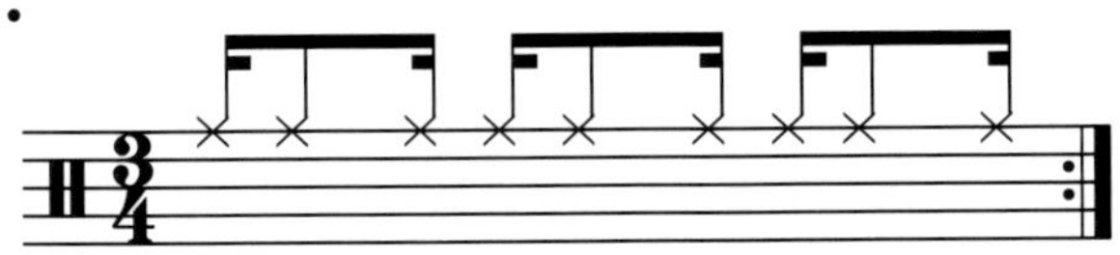

32.

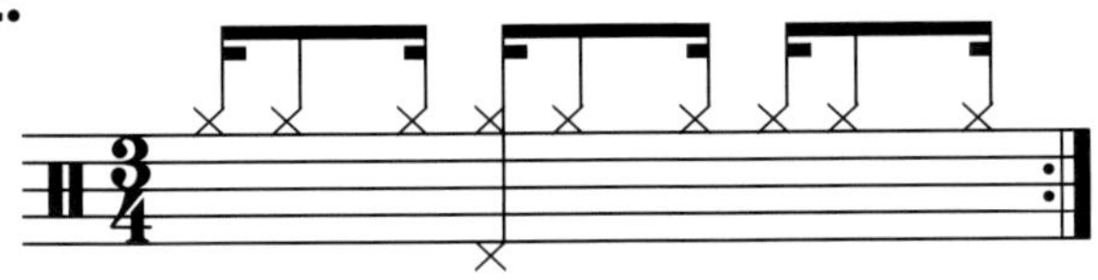

33.

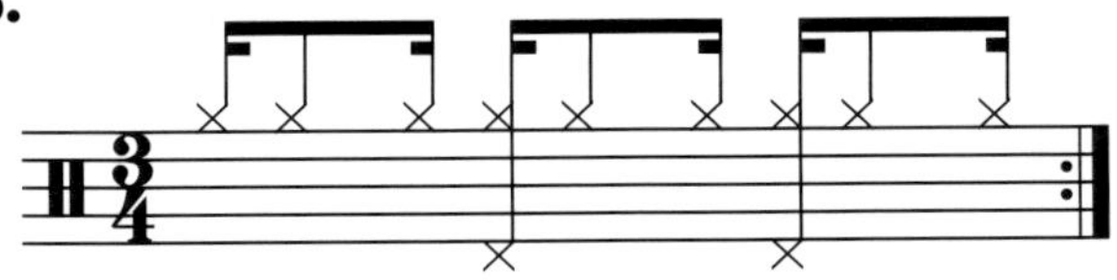

34.

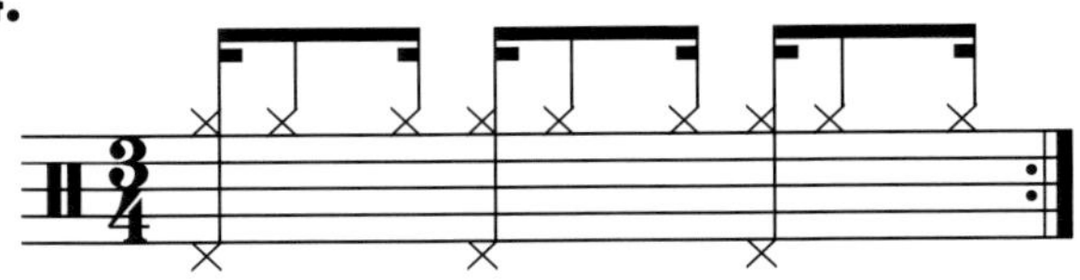

35.

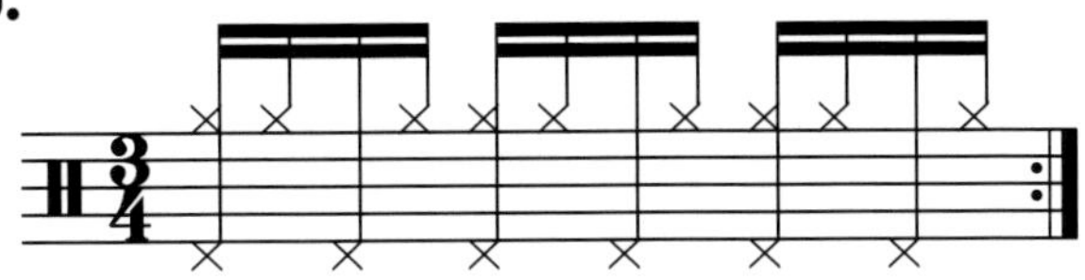

36.

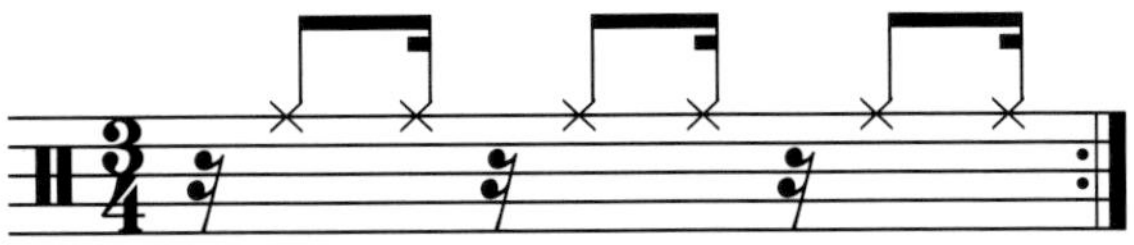

37.

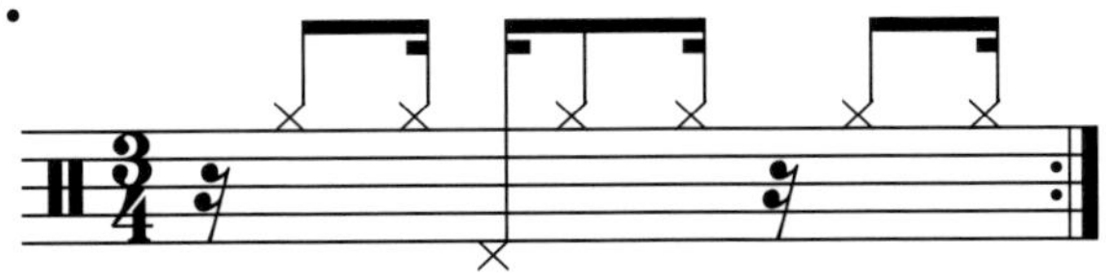

38.

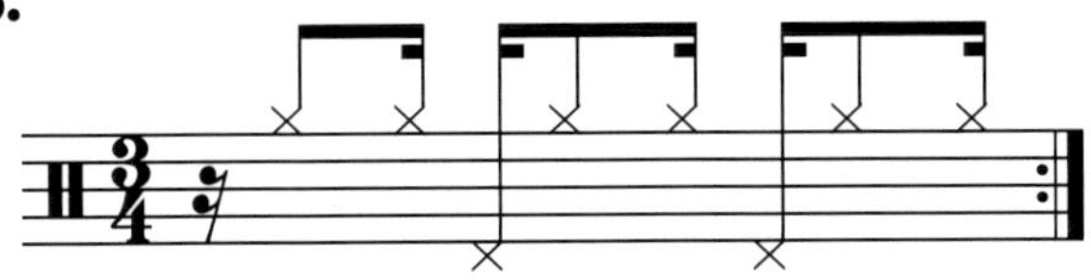

39.

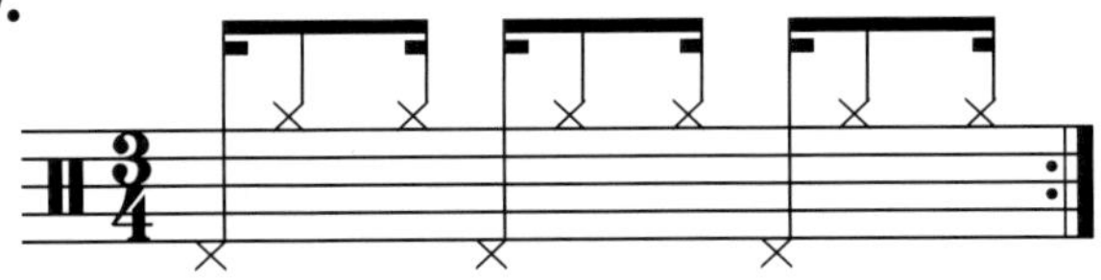

40.

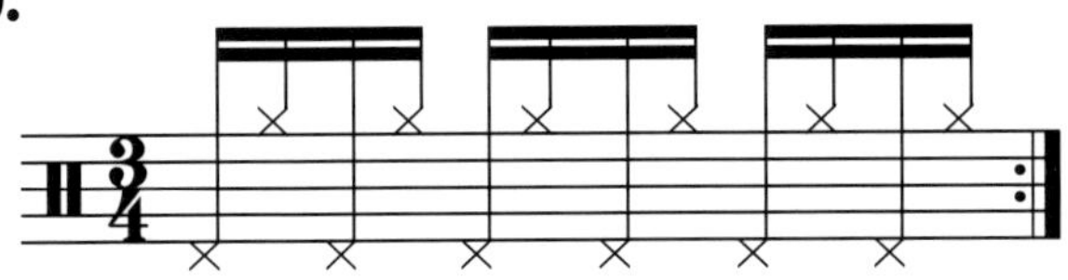

3/4 FLPs

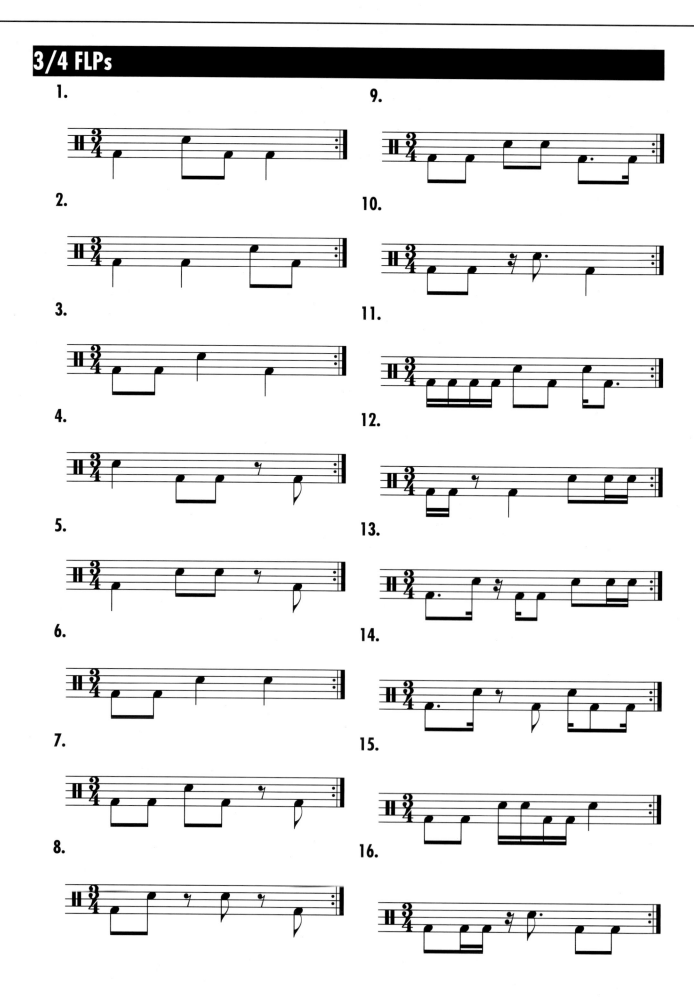

3/4 FLPs (continued)

17.

18.

19.

20.

21.

22.

23.

24.

25.

26.

27.

28.

29.

30.

31.

32.

33.

34.

35.

36.

37.

38.

39.

40.

Chapter 9

Fred's Musical Recommendations

The following is a list of songs and drummers I recommend that you study to develop a better understanding of the topics covered in this book. All of these artists have many recording credits, too many to list here. I encourage you to study as many recordings as possible by these and other artists.

The "Big One" Drummers

Clayton Fillyau (James Brown)
Melvin Parker (James Brown)

John "Jabo" Starks (James Brown)
Clyde Stubblefield (James Brown)

2 & 4 Pocket Drummers

Acuna, Alex
- BB Winans
- Andre Crouche

Baker, Michael
- Zawinul Syndicate
- Whitney Houston

Gaylor, Marcus
- Yellow Jackets

Bennette, Alvino
- L.T.D.

Bisquera, Curt
- Tom Petty
- Mick Jagger

Brown, Ollie
- Billy Preston (Will It Go Round in Circles)
- Rufus (Tell Me Something Good)
- The Jacksons (Triumph)

Brown, Gerry
- Stevie Wonder (Live)

Bryant, William Bubba
- Ronnie Laws
- The Crusaders
- Sam Riney
- George Howard

Cambell, Gordon

Campbell, Teddy

Chambers, Dennis
- John Scofield (Blue Matter)
- Parliament
- Funkadelic

- George Duke
- Stanley Clark Project

Chancler, Ndugu
- Michael Jackson
- The Meeting
- Herbie Hancock
- George Duke

Clark, Mike
- Herbie Hancock (Head Hunters)
- Brand X

Emory, Sonny
- Earth, Wind & Fire (Greatest Hits Live)
- Lee Ritenour (Alive in L.A.)
- Maze Featuring Frankie Beverly Back to Basics)

Ferrone, Steve
- Average White Band (Person to Person)
- Chaka Khan (Naughty)

Fisher, Andre
- Rufus

Fulwood, Tiki
- Funkadelic
- Miles Davis

Gadd, Steve
- Grover Washington (Winelight)
- Van McCoy
- Al Jarreau (Stuff Like That)

Gadson, James
- Marvin Gaye
- The Emotions
- Bill Withers

Garibaldi, David
- Tower of Power
- Denise Williams

Greene, Ed
- Barry White
- Diana Ross
- Smokey Robinson

Griffin, Rayford
- George Duke
- Anita Baker

Hakim, Omar
- Dave Grusin
- Joe Sample
- Madonna

Horton, Yogi
- Luther Vandross
- Ashford & Simpson

Humphrey, Paul
- Marvin Gaye
- Steely Dan

Johnson, Ralph
- Earth Wind & Fire
- The Emotions

Jordan, Steve

Kennedy, Will
- The Yellowjackets

Lawson, Ricky
- George Duke (Master of the Game) (Follow the Rainbow)
- Kenny Loggins (Leap of Faith)
- The Yellow Jackets (Mirage a Trois)
- Whitney Houston (I)
- Babyface (MTV Unplugged Live 1997)
- Steely Dan (Two Against Nature)

Mason, Harvey
- George Benson
- Lee Ritenour
- Dave Grusin
- Bob James
- Fourplay
- Marvin McQuitty
- Fred Hammond

Maxwell, Bill
- The Winans
- Andre Crouche
- Sandra Crouche
- Helen Baylor

McQuitty, Marvin
- Fred Hammond

Mouzon, Alphonse
- Tanacious Records
- Herbie Hancock
- Larry Coryell & the 11th House Band

Porcaro, Jeff
- The Four Tops (When She Was My Girl)
- Boz Scaggs (Silk Degrees & Down Two Then Left)
- Michael Jackson
- Toto

Pounds, Raymond
- Stevie Wonder

Purdie, Bernard
- Aretha Franklin
- Steely Dan

Richards, Land
- Gladys Knight
- Gerald Albright (Live at Birdland West)

Robinson, John
- Michael Jackson
- Rufus and Chaka Khan
- Anita Baker

Shapiro, Michael
- Keyvn Latteau
- Sergio Mendez

Smith, Marvin "Smith"
- Kevin Eubanks
- Steve Coleman

St. James, Tony
- Rodney Franklin
- Natalie Cole
- Maze

White, Fred
- Earth, Wind & Fire
- Donny Hathaway
- The Emotions
- Denise Williams

White, Lenny
- Twentynine
- Streamline

Wilburn, Vince
- Miles Davis

Williams, James "Diamond"
- Ohio Players

Zoro
- Bobby Brown
- Lenny Kravitz
- Jody Watley

The Time Movement Recommendations

Gerry Brown
- Stevie Wonder "Live"

"Love's in Need," "Rocket Love Golden Lady," "For Your Love"
  All of these tunes are played with a "behind the beat" feel.

"I Wish," "Superstition," "Signed Sealed Delivered," "Another Star"
  All of these tunes are played with a "little ahead of the beat" feel.

"Ribbon in the Sky," "Sir Duke"
  These tunes are played with a "straight down the middle of the beat" feel.

Sonny Emory
- Steely Dan (*Two Against Nature*, Track 9)
  On this track, the time is "right down the middle."

Steve Ferrone
- Average White Band (*Person to Person*)
  Listen to the track "Cloudy" (my favorite); Steve lays back on this track.

- Chaka Khan (*Naughty*)
  This is one of the best recorded drum tracks ever. Steve places the snare right down the middle on Tracks 1,3, and 5. Track 6 has a slight edge to it.

Ricky Lawson
- First Things First (Tracks 1, 2, 6, 10)
  Ricky plays right down the middle.

- First Things First (Tracks 3 and 4)
  Ricky plays behind the beat.

- First Things First (Tracks 5, 7, 8, 9, and 11)
  Ricky plays slightly behind the beat.

- Steely Dan (*Two Against Nature*, Track 1)
  Ricky plays on top of the beat.

Harvey Mason
- Dave Grusin (*Mountain*, Tracks 1 and 2)
  Harvey nails beats 2 and 4.

- George Benson (*In Flight; The World Is a Ghetto*)
  This track has an intense feel to it, and Harvey makes the listener feel it by giving the song an edge.

- Earl Klugh and Bob James (Tracks 2 and 6)
  These tracks are a little on the backside of the beat.

- Earl Klugh and Bob James (Track 7)
  This track is straight down the middle.

- Earl Klugh and Bob James (Tracks 4 and 8)
  These tracks are played a little on top.

- Fourplay (*Fourplay*, Tracks 1 and 2)
  Track 1 is a little on top; Track 2 is down the middle.

- Ratamacue (Tracks 1 and 3)
  These tracks are played right down the middle.

Michael White
- Steely Dan (*Two Against Nature*, Tracks 1 and 6)
  These tracks are played right down the middle.

- Maze featuring Frankie Beverly (*Back to Basics*, Track 1)
  This track is played with an edge that makes the listener feel the intensity of the lyrics.

CD Track Index

Disc 1

FOUR BARS OF SPACE
TRACK 75 SLOW TEMPO 70 BPM
TRACK 76 MEDIUM TEMPO 97 BPM
TRACK 77 FAST TEMPO 135 BPM

EIGHT BARS OF SPACE
TRACK 78 SLOW TEMPO 75 BPM
TRACK 79 MEDIUM TEMPO 108 BPM
TRACK 80 FAST TEMPO 146 BPM

MIDDLE CHANGES
TRACK 81 SLOW TEMPO 60 BPM
TRACK 82 MEDIUM TEMPO 80 BPM
TRACK 83 FAST TEMPO 127 BPM

TWO-BAR COUNT-OFFS
TRACK 84 SLOW TEMPO 62 BPM
TRACK 85 MEDIUM TEMPO 84 BPM
TRACK 86 FAST TEMPO 129 BPM

ONE-BAR COUNT-OFFS
TRACK 87 SLOW TEMPO 63 BPM
TRACK 88 MEDIUM TEMPO 100 BPM
TRACK 89 FAST TEMPO 136 BPM

TWO-BEAT COUNT-OFFS
TRACK 90 SLOW TEMPO 68 BPM
TRACK 91 MEDIUM TEMPO 98 BPM
TRACK 92 FAST TEMPO 133 BPM

ONE-BEAT COUNT-OFFS
TRACK 93 SLOW TEMPO 60 BPM (COUNT-OFFS)
TRACK 94 MEDIUM TEMPO 92 BPM
TRACK 95 FAST TEMPO 127 BPM
TRACK 96 PLAY-ALONG #2 SPACE BOOGIE WITH DRUMS
TRACK 97 PLAY-ALONG #2 SPACE BOOGIE MINUS DRUMS
TRACK 98 PLAY-ALONG #3 HOW DO YOU FILL? WITH DRUMS
TRACK 99 PLAY-ALONG #3 HOW DO YOU FILL? MINUS DRUMS

Disc 2

PLAYING THE HITS (DUE TO THE LIMITATION OF TIME ON THE CD, ALL HORN HIT TRACKS WERE RECORDED AT 110 BPM)
TRACK 1–48
TRACK 49 PLAY-ALONG #4 JUST HIT ME WITH DRUMS
TRACK 50 PLAY-ALONG #4 JUST HIT ME MINUS DRUMS

SET-UPS
TRACK 51 EXAMPLE #1 WITH DRUMS
TRACK 52 EXAMPLE #5 WITH DRUMS
TRACK 53 PLAY ALONG #5 HITSVILLE WITH DRUMS
TRACK 54 PLAY ALONG #5 HITSVILLE MINUS DRUMS

TIME MOVEMENT
PLAYING ON TOP
TRACK 55 SLOW TEMPO 74 BPM
TRACK 56 MEDIUM TEMPO 102 BPM
TRACK 57 FAST TEMPO 122 BPM

PLAYING IN THE MIDDLE OF THE BEAT
TRACK 58 SLOW TEMPO 74 BPM
TRACK 59 MEDIUM TEMPO 102 BPM
TRACK 60 FAST TEMPO 122 BPM

PLAYING BEHIND THE BEAT
TRACK 61 SLOW TEMPO 74 BPM
TRACK 62 MEDIUM TEMPO 102 BPM
TRACK 63 FAST TEMPO 122 BPM

PLAY-ALONG #6 EMOTIONS
TRACK 64 PLAY ALONG #6 EMOTIONS WITH DRUMS
TRACK 65 PLAY ALONG #6 EMOTIONS MINUS DRUMS

PLAY-ALONG #7 THE "TIME MAZE"
TRACK 66 THE "TIME MAZE" PLAY-ALONG WITH FRED DINKINS
TRACK 67 THE "TIME MAZE" MINUS DRUMS
TRACK 68 THE "TIME MAZE" WITH ARTIST: HARVEY MASON
TRACK 69 THE "TIME MAZE" WITH ARTIST: RICKY LAWSON
TRACK 70 THE "TIME MAZE" WITH ARTIST: CURT BISQUERA
TRACK 71 THE "TIME MAZE" WITH ARTIST: LAND RICHARDS
TRACK 72 THE "TIME MAZE" WITH ARTIST: DOANE PERRY
TRACK 73 THE "TIME MAZE" WITH ARTIST: GERRY BROWN
TRACK 74 THE "TIME MAZE" WITH ARTIST: DENNIS CHAMBERS

An extra-special thanks to the following companies for all of their support, fine products, and generosity toward this project.

remo.com

www.vater.com

Direct Sound

EXTREME ISOLATION

Headphones